VINTAGE VERMONT VILLAINIES

D1308081

Also by the author

They Died Crawling, and Other Tales of Cleveland Woe

The Maniac in the Bushes, and More Tales of Cleveland Woe

The Corpse in the Cellar, and Further Tales of Cleveland Woe

The Killer in the Attic, and More True Tales of Crime and Disaster from Cleveland's Past

Death Ride at Euclid Beach, and More Tales of Crime and Disaster from Cleveland's Past

Women Behaving Badly: True Tales of Cleveland's Most Ferocious Female Killers

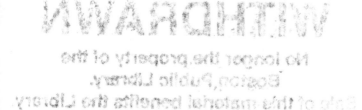

VINTAGE VERMONT VILLAINIES

True Tales of Murder & Mystery from the 19th & 20th Centuries

JOHN STARK BELLAMY II

The Countryman Press
Woodstock, Vermont

We welcome your comments and suggestions. Please contact Editor,
The Countryman Press, P.O. Box 748, Woodstock, VT 05091,
or e-mail countrymanpress@wwnorton.com. Those wishing to contact
the author directly may do so at his email: jstarkbi@tops-tele.com.

Eight of these stories originally appeared in more or less altered form in the *Vermont
Sunday Magazine,* a weekly supplement to the *Barre Montpelier Times Argus.*

Library of Congress Cataloging-in-Publication Data
Bellamy, John Stark.
Vintage Vermont villainies : true tales of murder & mystery from the 19th & 20th
centuries / John Stark Bellamy II. — 1st ed.
p. cm.
ISBN 978-0-88150-749-2 (alk. paper)
1. Murder—Vermont—History—19th century—Case studies. 2. Murder—
Vermont—History—20th century—Case studies. 3. Murder victims—Vermont—
Case studies. I. Title.

HV6533.V5B45 2007

364.152'309743—dc22

2007014448

Cover design by Honi Werner
Text design and composition by S. E. Livingston

Published by The Countryman Press, P.O. Box 748, Woodstock, Vermont 05091

Distributed by W. W. Norton & Company, Inc.,
500 Fifth Avenue,
New York, NY 10110

Printed in the United States of America

10 9 8 7 6 5 4 3 2 1

To Christopher Aladdin Bellamy,
dearest of brothers and the
one who showed the way to
the Green Mountain Eden

CONTENTS

PREFACE AND ACKNOWLEDGMENTS

Why a book about Vermont murders and kindred horrors? Well you might ask—as my mother did some fifteen years ago when I bashfully proffered to her my very first murder story. Imagine my surprise when that former Hearst newspaper reporter concluded her reading of it by exclaiming, "Why would you want to write about something like that?"

She had a good question, and I have devoted much thought to it in the years since, an interval during which I wrote approximately 130 murder and disaster stories collected in seven books and created a personal cottage industry of print, talks, and tours about the crimes and calamities of my native place, northeast Ohio. So why do I have so intense a passion for matters dolorous and dire?

There are many answers to that query, all of them valid. To begin with, I grew up in a newspaper family: My father was a third-generation journalist in the first decade of his half-century career when he met and married the aforesaid Hearst journalist in 1939. Thus I came of age in a family where it was not only considered normal to discuss the latest domestic homicide at the dinner table but even allowable to abruptly quit that place to chase the siren song of any fire engines that chanced to pass by. In short, such sensational subjects were considered perfectly acceptable entertainment, to be discussed and enjoyed with kith and kin. I have since learned that such appetite for narratives of human misbehavior and mischance is a near-universal one, as indicated by the unfailing success of crime-based books, motion pictures, and such enduring phenomena as O. J. Simpson, JonBenet Ramsey, and the like.

More personally, I have always been interested in the behavior of people under seemingly unbearable stress, a condition that tends to afflict most murderers and murderesses. Extreme states of mind tend to induce drastic modes of behavior, and I remain fascinated, if chronically puzzled, by the evil actions of the people I write about. Why some people cross the moral lines most of us observe, why they violate the norms most of us respect (little rules like not dismembering loved ones or killing them to accelerate one's inheritance) are questions I cannot answer. But I remain unapologetically captivated and hugely entertained by their violent misbehavior and their quirks of personality. Hence the guiding principle for the inclusion of each story here has been, above all, the personality of its chief protagonist. Truth is much stranger than fiction: I could never invent a killer so moronically demonic as Mary Rogers or contrive a slayer as complex as the amazing Frank C. Almy. Nor could I invent the unintended B-movie comedy of Chester's Catherine Packard puzzle, the enduring pathos of Paula Welden's vanishing on the Long Trail, or the Cagneyesque melodrama of the Springfield Weatherup tragedy. It is my pleasure to introduce such narratives to a contemporary audience, and I believe my readers will find them as compelling as I do.

Readers will note that all the stories in this book are at least fifty years old. The reasons for my focus on strictly vintage crimes, as in my past books, are twofold. The first reason is sheer delicacy: I do not wish to revive awful memories in the minds of those persons who were secondary victims of the crimes I chronicle. One of the things I have learned in writing about crime is that murder narratives mutate in nature over time. To those who experience murder firsthand, it is simply a tragedy; to those of the next generation, it survives in the nature of a family scandal; and for subsequent generations it is simply an entertaining story.

The other reason for my selection of older murders is sheer stylistic preference. As L. P. Hartley famously remarked, "The past is a foreign country; they do things differently there." As one with a pronounced antiquarian streak, I have ever been intrigued and charmed by the peculiarities of past manners, past speech, and past lifestyles. This fascination was the compelling motive behind my seven books on Ohio crime, and its application and relevance to Vermont, a state that has always had strong roots to its past, are obvious.

As a comparative newcomer to Vermont, I realize that my relative unfamiliarity with the region and its history may have rendered me vulnerable to committing errors of fact or interpretation that would be obvious to a Green Mountain State native. For any such errors I can only assume full responsibility and offer in exculpation the blunt apology of Dr. Samuel Johnson for like solecisms: "Ignorance, Madam, pure ignorance." Preemptively, in that regard, I would like to note that the spelling of Vermont surnames fluctuates with increasing novelty the further one goes back into its archives, annals, and newspapers.

One of the distinct pleasures of authorship is publicly thanking persons who have particularly helped in the creation of one's book. This volume would never have happened without the interest and encouragement of the editorial staff at the *Barre Montpelier Times Argus*, in whose pages many of these stories first appeared. I particularly wish to thank Deputy Editor Andrew Nemethy, who responded positively to my first submission there, and, most vehemently, Dirk VanSustern, whose editing of the stories and procurement of stunning pictorial matter added so much to their initial appearance in the *Vermont Sunday Magazine*. Others who gave much-appreciated aid to the making of this book include: the staff of the Vermont Department of Libraries in Montpelier, most especially Meg Page, Rita Robinson, and Paul Donovan; the staff of the Vermont Historical Society, most especially Marjorie Strong; the staff of the Aldrich Public Library in Barre, most especially library director Karen Lane; librarian Marie McAndrew-Taylor of the Blake Memorial Library in East Corinth; Bradford Public Library director Irene Mann and her staff; the staff of the Vermont Department of Health, Public Records Division, in Middlesex (thanks for lugging out all those humongous docket books!); the staff of the Special Collections Department at the Bailey/Howe Library at the University of Vermont in Burlington; Chester town clerk Deborah J. Aldrich, Chester town sexton Ken Barrett, and Andy Ojanen of the Chester Historical Society; Topsham town clerk–treasurer Juanita Clafin; and Orange County District Court deputy clerk Sabra Sutton and her wonderful staff in Chelsea. I would like to thank Howard Mosher for sharing his Vermont murder lore—and for being the best writer in the state. Thanks are due also to Vermont District Court judge Robert Bent and attorney Gavin Reed for suggesting two of the stories. Washington County Family Court judge Barney Bloom generously shared his knowledge of the Anna Wheeler and Gullivan murders, among other subjects. I also received much aid in locating prison records and threading the mazes of criminal law and research from Carmen Shalu, Cheryl Gates, John Perry, and Kerry DeWolfe. An enormous debt is owed to Glenn E. Novak, whose skillful editing of this book removed many infelicities in the original manuscript. Thanks also go to Avril McInally at the Cuyahoga County Public Library, who, as ever, speedily and painstakingly fulfilled all my reference queries. My greatest debt is to my wife, Laura Ann Serafin, whose love, support, and interest make this and all else worthwhile. Lastly, this book is dedicated to my brother, Christopher Aladdin Bellamy, with thanks for all his support, most especially in showing the way to this blessed state.

—John Stark Bellamy II
January 10, 2007

"THE MOST DIABOLICAL AND REVOLTING MURDER"

The 1880 Meaker Tragedy

Vermont has had its share of gothic sights. But few could rival in horror the scene on the Little River road out of Waterbury that cold midnight of April 27, 1880. A wakeful watcher in that darkness might have seen a horse-drawn buggy crawling up the road to Stowe. And if he were keen-eyed, he might have identified the buggy's two passengers, Washington County deputy sheriff Frank Atherton and Almon Meaker, the nineteen-year-old son of Duxbury farmer Horace C. Meaker.

They had been traveling for a couple of hours when Almon halted the rig near Deacon John White's farm and pointed toward the woodsy swamp at the side of the road. Atherton alighted from the buggy and waded into the mire, splashing a path about forty-five feet to a two-foot-deep pit of water. After kicking aside some covering branches, he knelt down and plunged his right arm into the water. Seconds later, he withdrew it. Clenched in his fist was the arm of nine-year-old Alice Meaker. Her dead body had lain hidden in that "muck pit" for almost exactly three days.

Atherton dragged the muddy corpse back to the buggy and

heaved it up onto the seat next to Almon Meaker. There was scant room there, and Atherton told Almon he would have to hold the corpse upright to keep it from falling off the buggy. It took almost three hours to take the body back to Alice's Duxbury home, and Almon whimpered with terror as he tightly embraced the corpse, his head on its shoulder. But it seemed only fair to Sheriff Atherton: after all, it was Almon who had helped put Alice Meaker in her watery grave.

The Meaker case was the most shocking crime of nineteenth-century Vermont. It truly was, as one of its earliest chroniclers termed it, "a most revolting murder," and one committed by two persons of "hellish malignity." That Emeline Meaker, a wife and a mother of three, should conceive and carry out a plan to murder her own foster child was horrifying enough. But that she had suborned her own son into helping her commit her satanic act seemed to go beyond received or even possible notions of the female sex itself. That unnatural aspect of the case, as much as the murder itself, would help hasten Emeline to her end on a Windsor Prison scaffold in 1883.

The Meaker tragedy began its germination thirteen years before. As now, the nineteenth century was a dangerous place for unwanted children, and Alice Meaker seems to have been one from her birth on August 25, 1870. Alice was the elder of two children born to Orrin Meaker and his third wife, Mary. Shortly after the birth of his son Henry ("Hilie") in 1873, Orrin died, leaving his family destitute. Soon after that, Alice and Hilie were placed in the Charlotte town poor farm. The official reason was that Mary Meaker abused her children; the real concern may have been doubts about Mary's chastity.

Alice and Hilie did not thrive during their half decade at the Charlotte poor farm. They were unhappy, and Alice, usually described as a "timid, shrinking" child, may have been the victim of a would-be rapist there. Poor-farm overseer Joseph Barton chose not to credit her rape accusation, characterizing her—after her death—as "an obstinate, cunning, mischievous, and disobedient child." But it's likely that, as Christina Perry, a chronicler of the Meaker tragedy, has argued, Barton's post-murder characterization may have been motivated by guilt over his role in Alice's ultimate fate.

Alice and Hilie's fortunes seemed to have finally taken a turn for the better in 1879. In exchange for $50, Horace C. Meaker, one of Orrin Meaker's sons by a previous marriage (making Horace the half-sibling of Alice and Hilie), agreed to take the two children into his family. On May 5, 1879, Horace posted a performance bond for their adoption and brought them to his Duxbury farm, where they joined Horace and Emeline's own children, Eleanor, 21, and Almon, 19.

After their previous sufferings, Alice and Hilie must have found their instant family too good to be true—and it was. Within days of the children's arrival, the Meaker neighbors began to take note of disquieting sights and sounds emanating from the Meaker residence. It wasn't just that Alice seemed terrified or that she was never seen at play. Several visitors would later testify at Emeline's murder trial that they had seen her whip Alice and beat her with a variety of domestic weapons, including a broom and a heavy stick. Sometimes Emeline even forced Alice to strip naked before her beatings. And Richard Thorndike, a farmer living across the river from the Meakers' "Mutton Hollow" tenant farm, testified that he could hear the screams of the two children half a mile away. Tellingly, nothing was done, even after Thorndike complained to authorities. One of the few perceptive contemporary observations on the social context of the Meaker murder was the community complicity noted by an unidentified journalist: "The interference of any individual, animated by the commonest feelings of humanity might have checked the development of the malignant passions that ripened into the murder of Alice Meaker."

Such interference was not to be. Emeline Meaker's abuse escalated after the family moved in March 1880 to a leased Duxbury farm of 212 acres owned by Joseph Somerville. Just two weeks after that, Emeline found her son Almon in the pantry alone while he was getting his lunch. Emeline told Almon that she couldn't stand having Alice around anymore and had decided to do away with her. She wanted him to take Alice out and abandon her to starve on a remote mountain (probably Mount Mansfield). Almon refused, sensibly suggesting that Emeline merely send Alice back to the poor farm. But Emeline was used to getting what she wanted from Almon, and she kept at him in the days that followed. Finally, on Tuesday, April 20, Almon gave in and agreed to her latest plan.

On Friday evening, April 23, Almon walked into William Carpenter's Waterbury drugstore and bought some butter plates. He also purchased fifteen grains of strychnine, telling Carpenter that he wanted to kill some rats in the buttery. Almon then walked over to Harley Bates's nearby livery stable, where he hired a black mare and buggy. He drove it home, where he waited outside for a few moments until Emeline and Alice appeared and climbed next to him on the seat. With her daughter Eleanor away and her husband Horace asleep, Emeline had taken Alice out through a back window, telling the sleepy child that they were going for a "ride."

Indeed they were. Driving the buggy steadily through the dark, Henry took it through Waterbury, heading north toward Stowe. Arriving at the top of the Sylvester Henry hill, he suddenly halted the rig. He pulled a bottle from his pocket, quickly mixed the strychnine powder with some sweetened water, and poured the mixture into a crockery mug, a gift from Mary Meaker to her daughter that bore the motto "Remember Me." It took little persuasion to make the unwary child drink of the sugary liquid, and the buggy soon resumed its route up the Stowe road.

Twenty minutes later the poison hit Alice hard. Rocking violently in convulsions, she repeatedly screamed, "Mother! Mother! Mother!" even as Emeline tried to smother her cries by clamping her hands over Alice's mouth. Her death paroxysms lasted some minutes, eventually forcing Almon to park the buggy on a covered bridge, which he hoped would muffle her shrieks. Finally it was over, and time to hide the body. After driving another four miles toward Stowe, Almon stopped the buggy and dragged Alice's corpse into the swampy thicket. He tied a sack around her head, then shoved her into a watery hole and covered it up with some wood lying around. By the time he staggered out of the woods, Alice probably looked as she appeared when Atherton fished her out three nights later: a little girl clad in a red calico dress and apron, a chemise, drawers, a blue cloak, shoes, and colored stockings—with mud in her hair and mouth. Driving back to Waterbury in the wee hours, the killers threw the incriminating water bottle into the river. Then Almon dropped off Emeline at home, returned the rig to Harley Bates, and began hoping for the best.

Whatever their moral defects, it is inarguable that Emeline and Almon Meaker were about the most incompetent murderers on record. Notwithstanding their forethought about the mechanics of the murder, they had not even worked out a mutual cover story or alibi. So when their landlord Joseph Somerville remarked on Alice's absence the next day, Emeline and Almon immediately began spouting improbable and contradictory explanations for the girl's disappearance. Emeline said she had run away in the middle of the night. No, countered Almon, he had taken her to a party in Moscow and had subsequently dropped her off at the home of a friend.

His suspicions aroused, Somerville consulted with Duxbury town officials Eber Huntley and Jacob Foss. Their interrogation of Emeline and Almon only elicited more contradictory stories, including Emeline's shocking comment that no one should "spend a cent" looking for her foster child. Increasingly alarmed by Emeline and Almon's obvious prevarications and worried about growing public suspicions of foul play, Huntley and Foss finally contacted Washington County deputy sheriff Frank Atherton on Monday, April 26. Surmising quickly that Emeline and Almon had done away with Alice, Atherton endured several hours of Emeline's evolving explanations before going to work on the obvious weak link, the submissive Almon. Late that evening, Almon cracked, blurting out the details of what he and his mother had done to Alice. Returning with Atherton to his mother, he said, "Mother, I have told the whole truth, nothing is kept back." Emeline immediately embraced him and murmured, "My darling boy." Turning to Atherton, she begged him not to take Almon away, as she was the guilty party.

Minutes later, Atherton and Almon were on their way to the swampy woods on the Stowe road. Arrested the next morning, Emeline and Almon were immediately arraigned before Justice William Dillingham, charged with murder, and taken to the Washington County Jail in Montpelier. Their incarceration came not a moment too soon, for there was already angry talk in Washington County towns of lynching them both.

As expected, the seven-day trial of the Meakers in November 1880 offered a generous quota of sensationalism. But it also featured some legal peculiarities and developments unanticipated by both sides. To begin with, Almon Meaker had repudiated his original confession. He now claimed that he, and he alone, had planned and committed the murder of Alice Meaker. Obviously desperate to shield his dominating mother, he now apparently offered himself as a judicial victim in her stead. Following the selection of their jury on November 22 and Judge Timothy P. Redfield's refusal to allow them separate trials, Almon stunned everyone in the courtroom by pleading guilty to first-degree murder. He was instantly returned to jail, and the prosecutors, state's attorney Frank Plumley and his assistant William P. Dillingham, began constructing the legal noose for Emeline Meaker's neck.

It wasn't a difficult task. Over the next seven days, fifty-three witnesses offered devastating testimony against Emeline Meaker. The state began by proving the facts of Alice's death. After several physicians described the details of her autopsy, University of Vermont chemist R. August Whitthaus delivered his expert opinion that Alice had died of strychnine poisoning. The subsequent testimony of druggist Carpenter linked the poison to Almon, and Harley Bates told the jury the circumstances of Almon's hiring his rig and returning it early on the morning of April 24.

Half a dozen witnesses next shared graphic memories of how Emeline had repeatedly whipped and beaten Alice. Neighbor Flora Drugg recalled seeing Emeline whipping Alice and calling her a "little bitch." Then several witnesses recalled seeing a man, woman, and child in the Bates livery rig in the Waterbury area on April 23. These witnesses couldn't identify the trio, but then Susan Pickett took the stand. She was well acquainted with the Meaker family and told the jury that she had seen Almon, Emeline, and Alice in the Bates buggy at about 8:45 PM on the murder night. Charles H. Heath, Hiram Carleton, and Edwin F. Palmer, Emeline's defense counsel, tried hard to shake Pickett on cross-examination but without avail. Nor could they soften the horror of Mrs. Linn A. Foster's recollections. Mrs. Foster had been up late that night, nursing her children—and she lived only fifty feet from where the buggy had stopped when the poison hit Alice. Foster vividly remembered hearing the sound of a horse and buggy, followed by a child's anguished voice crying, "Mother! Mother! Mother!" Mrs. Betsey Myndrt followed Foster and recounted how she had heard the sounds of a horse and buggy on a covered bridge near her home—and the voices of two persons trying to quiet a third in some kind of distress.

Interestingly, the most potentially dangerous witness against Emeline did not testify. The prosecutors wanted to put Hilie Meaker on the stand but were prevented by an alarmed Judge Redfield, who did not want a capital case decided by a child's testimony. Moreover, Hilie's testimony was hardly needed, after the devastating examinations of Deputy Sheriff Atherton and Washington County jailer D. W. Dudley. Atherton recounted in damning detail his investigation of Alice's disappearance, fully cataloging Emeline's clumsy prevarications and hysterical admissions. Dudley followed with a narrative of Emeline's chronic jailhouse misbehavior, which included assaulting him and his deputies, setting her cell on fire, and trying to bribe her way out of jail via a blizzard of pleading, illiterate letters, which she threw out her cell window.

Emeline's defense, such as it was, opened on Friday afternoon, November 26. Several persons from Emeline's remote past first testified as to her respectable character. The next morning Emeline herself took the stand. It was a remarkable spectacle, and not just because of the unusual personality of the accused and her stake in the trial. As everyone in that courtroom knew, Emeline Meaker was almost completely deaf. Any questions asked of her had to be written out for her on a slate. Her painstaking examination by Charles Heath took most of the day but added nothing to the evidence. Indeed, most of her testimony seemed contrived merely to evoke pity in her jury. And it *was* a sad story. Married at eighteen to the older and feckless Horace, Emeline had endured twenty-three years of hardscrabble life on a half-dozen farms in as many Vermont towns. But as to the charges against her, Emeline offered only categorical denials, rather than an exculpatory alibi. All she knew about it, she told the jury, was that Alice was gone when she woke up on the morning of April 24. Confronted with the testimony of Frank Atherton about her many lies, Emeline swore that she couldn't remember what she had done or said during her interrogation on April 26.

William Dillingham commenced the closing arguments with a careful recitation of the circumstantial evidence against Emeline. Emphasizing the background of her persistent cruelty to Alice, he focused on connecting the elements of motive, means, and opportunity to the accused. After stressing the importance of Susan Pickett's eyewitness testimony that Emeline had been in the murder buggy—not at home as she claimed—he finished with a narrative of Alice's final minutes that left most of his courtroom audience in tears.

Thanks to her continuing bad behavior and lack of an alibi, Emeline's defense team didn't have much to work with—and their final arguments displayed the depth of their legal desperation. Edwin F. Palmer's plea largely ignored the evidence and mounted an abstract attack on Dillingham's inductive reasoning. Waxing more personal by the moment, Palmer insisted that Mrs. Pickett was simply mistaken in her identification and that Charles Armington and Cliff Drugg, two minor witnesses, were untrustworthy "half-breed Indians." He ended his choleric rant with an attack on his own client, characterizing Emeline Meaker as a creature too crazy and too deaf to be believed.

Carleton Heath's defense plea continued down the low road taken by Palmer. Abusing many of the state witnesses, he came down hard on Frank Atherton, pillorying him as a partisan lawman determined to frame Emeline Meaker. Pushing the limits of the jury's credulity, Heath insisted that Emeline Meaker had never mistreated little Alice, much less had a hand in her death. More soberly, Heath emphasized the lack of any obvious motive Emeline could have had for killing Alice. He closed by underlining inconsistencies in the timing of events by state witnesses and turned Emeline's deafness to her advantage by claiming that she was so hard of hearing that someone could have easily kidnapped Alice out of her home without her realizing it.

Frank Plumley's closing argument for the state set the seal of doom on Emeline Meaker. After deploring Heath's attacks on state witnesses, he reiterated the awful details of the crime and ended with the harsh estimation of Emeline Meaker that had become the substance of all journalistic accounts of her character: that she was not really even a woman, and should not be treated with the chivalry normally due her sex. Recalling her stolid reaction when Alice's body was brought back to the Meaker home, Plumley roared,

"[If] she had had any of the woman in her nature, wouldn't she at least have shown some emotion of affection and pity when the dead body was brought back into the house? But there is no proof that she exhibited any sign of emotion or feeling."

Following Judge Redfield's careful instructions, the jury went out at 6:15 PM on Tuesday, November 30. They returned just one hundred minutes later at 7:55 with a verdict. At 8:12 PM Emeline was led back to the courtroom, and Washington County clerk of courts Melville Smilie asked the jury for its verdict. "Guilty," replied jury foreman H. L. Kenyon, and all eyes in the courtroom turned to the prisoner.

It was yet another horrible scene in the macabre Meaker tragedy. Owing to her deafness, Emeline did not hear the verdict. First she stared inquisitively at the jury, then at her lawyers. Receiving no response, she looked at Judge Redfield. Finally, Redfield asked her lawyers to give her the bad news. They declined and suggested that Smilie tell her. Commanded by Redfield, Smilie wrote on a slip of paper, "The verdict of the jury is murder in the first degree," and handed it to her. She still didn't get it, until Charles Heath wrote something, which she finally understood. Shrieking with terror, she collapsed and gave vent to hysterical tears, even as she was enveloped in a mob of curious, insensitive spectators.

As expected, Emeline's lawyers appealed her conviction to the Vermont Supreme Court. Their chief complaints were that Judge Redfield had denied Emeline's request for a separate trial and that Almon had been allowed to exercise three peremptory challenges of prospective jurors over her protests. But on November 19, 1881, Emeline's death sentence was upheld by the high court. Speaking for the court, Justice Jonathan Ross ruled that the right to a separate trial was at the discretion of the presiding judge and that Emeline's right to challenge jurors did not include the right to choose them.

Unlike most capital cases in Vermont history, there was no organized public campaign to commute Emeline Meaker's death sentence. From the moment she was accused of murder, she was unremittingly vilified as an unnatural monster, a veritable libel on her sex. Newspaper accounts of the Alice Meaker case repeatedly echoed such pejorative language, calling Emeline a "virago," "an unnatural mother," a "repulsive looking" creature, and a "woman of masculine force" who was "strong and muscular."

Emeline's prospects weren't helped by her son Almon. After posing for two and a half years as the dutiful son taking the rap for his beloved mama, Almon eventually caved on October 10, 1882, four months before his scheduled execution. Confessing to prison officials, he admitted his part in Alice's murder but insisted it was all his mother's idea. The nearest he came to remorse was this memorably craven sentence: "I will say here that if I had thought [Alice's] death would have been so terrible, I never could have consented to aid her." As expected, Almon's supine deed paid off the following month when the Vermont legislature commuted his death sentence to life in prison.

Emeline Meaker died as she had lived, with little exterior emotion and much seething vindictiveness. Most of her two years in the Windsor Prison were spent feigning insanity, an act that consisted mainly of marathon screaming. As the last weeks of her life ebbed away, however, she calmed down and accepted her fate, albeit with much bitterness, especially toward Almon, whom she saw and kissed good-bye the day before her execution. She insisted once more that his lies had sent her to the gallows and that he would repent for them on his deathbed.

Emeline's final appearance was one of her better moments. Dressed in a new cambric dress sewn for her by Windsor Prison matron S. J. Durkee, Emeline was noticeably pale but marched with a firm step to the prison gallows, mounting its stairs as 125 avid spectators watched. She sat in a chair as Sheriff Atherton handed her a slip of paper, asking that she state any reason why she should not be executed. In a voice that could barely be heard, she said, "May God forgive you all for hanging me, an innocent woman." Gesturing toward a deputy, she continued, "I am as innocent as that man standing there."

The final moment had come. Her ankles were pinioned, and as the black hood was pulled over her face she could be heard whispering, "O Christ! O Christ!" Aware of her violent trembling, a compassionate deputy signaled Sheriff Rollin Amsden, who hit the spring for the drop. A second later, at 1:30 PM, March 30, 1883, Emeline Meaker hurtled eight feet to her death. Her neck was instantly broken, and she was pronounced dead twelve minutes later. Her corpse hung an additional eighteen minutes before it was cut down and buried in the Windsor Prison potter's field. Emeline's last request was to be buried in the family plot at Duxbury, but Horace had been cowed by public objections to her being buried next to her victim.

That was the official end of the Meaker story, although one great mystery still remains. As noted by Carleton Heath, no one was ever able to articulate a clear motive as to why Emeline killed Alice Meaker. A secondary mystery is why Almon Meaker risked his own life aiding his mother's monstrous scheme.

There *is* one possible explanation as to why both mother and son risked their lives to eliminate an otherwise insignificant and harmless little girl. It would also provide an explanatory subtext for the unanimous public perception of Emeline Meaker as an *unnatural* mother who deserved to die. That explanation surfaced briefly in a news account of Emeline's hanging, published four days later in the *Montpelier Argus & Patriot*. It is only fitting that I end this retelling of an antique tale with the whisper of a possible scandal that its contemporary audience might have considered even *worse* than Alice Meaker's murder. Quoth the *Argus & Patriot*:

> The only reason for this awful crime that could be suspected was that the mother and son had been living in incestuous relations, and that Alice knew of the fact; and that as she was in a day or two to leave their house and go to live with a neighbor, they feared she might tell their guilty secret.

CHAPTER 2

"WHAT SINISTER MOTIVE . . ."

The Murder of Joseph Felch

The rhythms of a Vermont rural spring have changed little since the first farmers arrived in the 1760s. Joseph Felch's last day of life, April 22, 1916, was a perfect paradigm of such patterns. Arising at 5 AM on that Saturday before Easter Sunday, the thirty-two-year-old farmer walked to his barn and tended his livestock. He spent the rest of his day in arduous toil at his two farms just about a mile and a half out of Waits River, a small village astride the stream of the same name that flows into the Connecticut River at Bradford, twelve miles away.

Joe returned home about 6 PM. After having supper with his wife, Anna, he announced that he was going to his sugarhouse, about a half-mile away through the woods. It was the end of the sugaring season, and Joe wanted to boil down his last sap run. He told Anna he didn't expect to be gone long, grabbed a newspaper to read during the tedious boiling process, and walked out into the rainy, overcast night.

Several hours went by. Shortly after 9 PM, Anna finished her chores and prepared for bed. About 11 PM, she called out to the hired girl, Josephine Pero, in the adjoining bedroom. Would Josephine mind sleeping in the same bed with her? Although Anna offered no reason for her unusual request, Josephine assented, and the two women bundled together for the night.

Anna awakened at five the next morning. Seeing no sign of Joe, she sent her seven-year-old daughter Bernice along with Josephine to look for him in the barn. He was not there, but Josephine and Bernice did see Otis Williams there, the twenty-one-year-old farmhand who lived with his wife in a cottage on Joe Felch's second farm. Williams told them that he hadn't seen Joe that morning and that Joe hadn't performed his usual early morning chores in the barn. When Josephine and Bernice returned to Anna with this news, the three of them immediately set out for the sugarhouse to find Joseph Felch.

Josephine would later recall that Anna seemed a little weepy as they approached the sugarhouse door. When they got there, an obviously reluctant Anna asked Josephine if she would go in first. Entering, Josephine saw Joseph Felch lying facedown on the floor near a small bench. His body and clothing were bloody, and he was lying atop a rifle. Anna was right behind Josephine and, seeing her husband, called to him three times. There was no response, and the three females fled the sugarhouse in terror.

After running to the nearby house of Anna's uncle, Thomas Smith, the distraught women babbled out the news of what they had found in the sugarhouse. Smith immediately telephoned physician William R. Rowland of East Corinth, and Topsham town health officer George Hight. The two men soon arrived at the sugarhouse, which was already thronged by a large crowd of curious spectators. Examining the body, Dr. Rowland quickly concluded that Joseph Felch had been dead for some hours. Judging from the position of his corpse and other physical circumstances, Rowland ruled out the likelihood of suicide. It seemed clear that Joseph had been sitting on a bench reading a newspaper when a bullet crashed through his head. It was also apparent that the fatal slug had been fired through a small crevice bored through an outside wall near the door. That slug had smashed through his left temple, broken his jaw, blown half his brains out, and then exited through his right temple before neatly drilling the glass chimney of a kerosene lantern hanging near his head and embedding itself in a wooden post. The skull damage indicated that death had been instantaneous. But how that death had occurred was less obvious. The rifle beneath Joe's corpse suggested suicide, but its size and right-angled position to the body made that hypothesis unlikely. The absence of powder burns on the corpse indicated that the fatal bullet had been fired at least four feet from the victim. And a trail of bloodstains on the floor hinted that the body had been moved after death. The bloodstained syrup can found next to the corpse supported that suspicion: The bloodstains were on the side of the can facing *away* from the corpse. After talking to Anna Felch and others at the scene, Dr. Rowland notified Orange County state's attorney Frank S. Williams that he had a suspicious death on his hands.

Williams's investigation that afternoon confirmed Dr. Rowland's misgivings. Before leaving the sugarhouse, Williams sent the corpse to the Waits River schoolhouse for an autopsy and asked Vermont state pathologist Dr. Bingham H. Stone and his assistant Dr. Charles Whitney to perform it. After calling in photographer Fred L. Adams of Bradford to photograph the murder scene, Williams scheduled an inquest and began interviewing friends and family of the deceased.

Once he decided it was murder, Williams quickly zeroed in on a couple of suspects. The victim's family and friends agreed that Joseph Felch had not had any known enemies. Ergo, there had to be some sinister, powerfully personal motive behind his brutal assassination. Whatever his initial suspicions, Frank Williams's inquiries were soon tightly focused on the seemingly fishy behavior of the widowed Anna Felch and her husband's farmhand, Otis Williams.

Some persons had already concluded that Anna Felch seemed insufficiently grieved by the death of her husband. She didn't seem to cry much, and several observers were struck by her repeated claims that her husband must have committed suicide, notwithstanding the contrary evidence in the sugarhouse. When Rowland first told Anna her husband was dead, she immediately blurted out that Joe had been working too hard, was physically run down, and must have killed himself. Try as he might, Dr. Rowland could not convince Anna otherwise; she repulsed all his arguments with the repeated phrase, "Oh yes, Dr. Rowland, he did."

Otis Williams's behavior seemed even more disquieting. It was soon disclosed that it was his .40-65 caliber rifle lying under Joe Felch's body. When he joined the crowd milling about Anna Felch's house late Sunday morning, the first thing Anna said to him was to inquire whether he had taken his rifle home with him the previous night. The obviously nervous Otis made repeated statements that day and the next that he feared he would be blamed for his employer's death. Indeed, he told Anna's brother Fred that he was already "the same as in the electric chair."

Frank Williams didn't wait long to pounce. Otis Williams was arrested as he was preparing to attend Joe Felch's funeral on Wednesday, April 26. Following a preliminary hearing in Bradford, he was jailed that same day in the Orange County Jail in Chelsea on suspicion of murder.

The world of 1916 was a different one from the present, especially when it came to the rights of the accused—and Otis Williams's treatment was not out of the ordinary. Insisting on his innocence, he was soon joined at the Orange County Jail by a Mr. Jackson, a self-confessed miscreant who went by the sobriquet of "Three-Fingered Jack." It didn't take the glib Jackson long to worm his way into the confidence of Otis Williams. Boasting of his own criminal exploits, Jackson encouraged Williams to confide in him and promised to help him escape from his predicament. The outcome of such suasions came on Sunday, May 7, when Otis Williams told Frank Williams he wished to make a confession. Otis was subsequently absent from his cell most of that day, but after he returned, Jackson told another prisoner, "The boy owned it all up and told the whole story." Several hours later, Jackson himself disappeared, without explanation. The following day he was replaced by a Mr. Arlen, who immediately took up with the pliable Otis where Jackson had left off. Spurred by Arlen's encouragement, Otis made another confession two days later and then accompanied lawmen to his Waits River cottage, where he retrieved a concealed morphine bottle. As soon as Otis returned to jail, his new friend Arlen, like Mr. Jackson, disappeared without explanation.

Anna Felch was arrested and jailed shortly after Otis's second confession. After hearing the testimony of several witnesses, an Orange County grand jury indicted Otis Williams and Anna Felch on first-degree murder charges on June 14. After consulting with legal counsel, the two defendants insisted on separate trials. The relevant criminal justice officials agreed without protest, hoping that a successful prosecution of Otis Williams would expedite Anna's conviction.

Joseph Felch's murder was by far the most sensational homicide in Orange County history. The trial of Otis Williams attracted commensurate attention, and the Orange County Courthouse chamber in Chelsea was crowded as the Williams trial got under way at 2 PM on July 17, 1916. Its proceedings also drew proportionate legal talent, with Vermont attorney general Herbert G. Barber and state's attorney Williams prosecuting for the state, and state senator David S. Conant and Stanley C. Wilson of Chelsea defending. The trial judge was Zed E. Stanton. His first act was to preside at the formal arraignment of both Otis Williams and Anna Felch. Anna greeted Otis with a smile but seemed nervous. Otis remained calm and was the cynosure of all eyes in his black cashmere suit. Following her arraignment, Anna returned to her county jail cell, while her lawyers remained in court to monitor developments that might hinder or help her subsequent defense.

Considering the notoriety of Joseph Felch's murder, the selection of the Williams jury was not unduly prolonged or ferociously contested. A circumstance compelling brevity was the summer heat, which soon became excruciating for the 250 to 300 persons packed into Judge Stanton's courtroom. The opposing sides used only one peremptory challenge apiece, and the rejected prospective jurors were excused for the usual reasons: health considerations, opposition to capital punishment, or an admitted reluctance to convict on the basis of circumstantial evidence.

Attorney General Barber's opening statement made it clear that the state would largely rely on circumstantial evidence to convict Otis Williams and Anna Felch of premeditated murder. Barber told the jury how Otis Williams had first come to work for Joseph Felch in August of 1915. Notwithstanding his marriage to young Mary Williams, Barber continued, Williams had soon commenced an adulterous affair with Anna Felch after he and Mary moved into a cottage on Felch's second farm. Their adultery had continued, Barber told the jury, right up until the night of Joseph's murder. Touching on motive, Barber asserted that the growing marital frictions aroused in the Felch and Williams families by the adultery had come to a head when Anna discovered in February 1916 that she was pregnant.

Moving on to the night of the murder, Barber claimed that Otis had met Anna at her home shortly after her husband left for his sugarhouse. Taking Otis's rifle with them, they walked to the sugarhouse. And when they got there, one of them put the barrel of the rifle up to the crevice in the wall and shot a bullet through Joseph Welch's head. Barber concluded that it had been a simple murder of elimination: Anna and Otis had killed Joseph so that they could be together. Holding its fire, the defense answered Barber's opening indictment by asking the jury to keep in mind the presumption of Williams's innocence before hearing the evidence against him.

The state's first witnesses showcased the forensic evidence against Williams. The jury was shown photographs, diagrams, and maps of the murder locale. Then state pathologist Dr. Bingham H. Stone and his assistant Dr. Charles Whitney described their postmortem, thoroughly demolishing any notion that Felch's death could have been a suicide.

Having established that Joseph Felch had definitely been murdered, prosecutors Barber and Williams elucidated a motive for the jury. A pathetic Mary Williams was forced to testify that her husband's adultery had caused "difficulties" in her marriage and that she and Otis had temporarily separated in November of 1915.

The next two trial days were largely consumed with tedious but critical wrangling over the admissibility of Otis Williams's two jailhouse confessions. The defense vociferously objected to their admission, arguing that they had been elicited under false pretenses, procured in the absence of legal counsel, and extorted by deceptive promises of leniency. Defense attorneys Conant and Wilson knew that his confessions were the most damaging evidence against Otis, and they were further incensed by the fact—cheerfully admitted by state's attorney Williams—that private detectives had been employed to elicit those confessions. Otis's sympathetic jailhouse pals, "Jackson" and "Arlen," it was now disclosed, had actually been operatives hired from the H. W. Morgan detective agency in Boston. But Sheriff Lawrence Welch and Frank Williams were able to convince Judge Stanton that they had not used threats or false promises to induce Williams's confessions and that he had been properly cautioned before making and signing them. On Saturday morning Stanton ruled the confessions admissible but persuaded the state to withhold them until Monday, so as not to prolong the weekend session.

By the time the confessions were admitted, Otis Williams's fortunes were already declining. While waiting for Stanton's ruling on the confessions, Otis's jury listened to Dr. William Rowland recount some rather more intimate confessions made to him by Otis Williams. Their first conversation had occurred on October 10, 1915, when Dr. Rowland was called to assist at the birth of Mary Williams's first child. Late that night Otis had told Rowland that he had been having "improper relations" with Anna Felch for some time. Indeed, Otis continued, they were so smitten that they planned to run away together soon to Meredith, New Hampshire, where Otis had relatives.

Apparently, the elopement plans of the adulterous conspirators had not worked out, for it was a disappointed Otis Williams that Dr. Rowland encountered a month later on November 9. Williams then recounted how he had sold his possessions, abandoned his wife, and gone to New Hampshire to wait for Anna. But she had never shown up and he was now returning to find out why.

Stanley Wilson's cross-examination of Rowland only dug the pit deeper for his client. His sarcastic queries to Dr. Rowland as to why he had not told Joseph Felch of Otis's October 10 confession only evoked the predictable self-justification of the doctor-patient relationship. And Otis's character was further besmirched when Wilson drew from Rowland the recollection that Otis had told him Joseph Felch was the "kindest, best boss" he'd ever had. The only helpful testimony Wilson squeezed out of Rowland was his judgment that Otis was "more or less below average, psychologically queer and not quite normal."

No less hurtful to Williams was the testimony of Sheriff Welch. The indiscreetly loquacious Williams had also confessed to him, admitting his illicit relations and recalling two separate occasions on which Anna had offered him cash to kill her husband.

Following these devastating disclosures, court stenographer Erwin Worthley read Otis Williams's two confessions aloud to the jury on Monday afternoon. The most important revelations were contained in the May 7 confession, in which Williams had sketched the history of his involvement with Anna Felch. It was Anna, he insisted, who initiated and accelerated their sexual liaison. It was Anna, he swore, who had contrived the idea of running away together, a scheme aborted by her failure to sell her possessions. It was Anna, too, Otis asserted, who had introduced the notion of killing her husband. And it was she who had induced Otis to procure the morphine, which she had poured into her husband's tea. When that failed, she had offered him $200, then $1,000, to kill Joe.

On Saturday, April 15, Otis's confession continued, Joe had asked Otis to get his rifle so they could shoot woodchucks. Otis had brought it, and on Friday night, April 21, he had cleaned the rifle and put it behind a separator. Anna had seen it there and took it out on Saturday and shot at targets with it. Before Otis left work that day, Anna told him to come back after supper. When he returned that night, Anna already had her red sweater and rubbers on. She also had the rifle in her hand, and she insisted that Otis accompany her to the sugarhouse.

Otis stated in his confession that he thought Anna was bringing the rifle to her husband. If so, he must have been much surprised when they got to the sugarhouse and Anna demanded that Otis shoot Joe through the hole in the wall. A shocked Otis repeatedly refused, whereupon Anna knelt by the crevice, poked the rifle through it, and shot her husband dead. Afterward, she sent Otis crawling through a hole in the wall to move her husband's body a few feet and place the rifle under it. They then returned to Anna's house and spent some more time together before Otis went home. One must surmise what ensued in the interval, as the gamier portions of Williams's confessions were deleted from newspaper accounts as "unprintable." Following Worthley's reading of them, the state tried to get hired girl Josephine Pero to give evidence of her mistress's adultery. But the best Josephine could offer was the tepid memory that she had once seen Otis exit a hayloft, followed minutes later by a furtive-looking Anna. After the testimony of some minor witnesses, the state rested its case against Otis Williams on Tuesday morning, July 25.

The state had consumed the better part of seven court days in presenting its case. The defense managed to get through its mere six witnesses that Tuesday afternoon. Wilson and Conant had apparently given up any idea of attacking Otis's confessions directly, so they simply called Frank Williams and Orange County jailer George Tracy to heap scorn on them for using detectives to inveigle confessions out of the gullible Otis Williams. More helpfully, Charles Ricker of Groton testified that Otis had been talking about leaving Felch's employ and coming to Ricker's farm in May. Farmer Ernest Bailey of Orange then corroborated the content of Ricker's conversations with Otis Williams. Last came John Felch, the sorrowing father of the murder victim. He testified simply that he knew of no trouble between his son and Otis Williams before the murder. John provided the most moving testimony of the trial, as he tearfully recalled the moment he knelt by his son's corpse sobbing, "Speak to me, Joe! Speak to me!"

The prosecution's closing arguments mainly reiterated the circumstantial evidence in the case: The physical circumstances of the sugarhouse precluded any scenario but murder, and Joseph Felch's killers had taken pains to stage a "suicide." The only persons with any likely motive were Anna Felch and Otis Williams, a motive well documented by Williams's sordid confessions.

Wilson and Conant's closing defense arguments surprised everyone by conceding the validity of much of Williams's confessions. Yes, the confessions gave ample evidence of an indefensible adultery, and it was admitted that Otis had been at least an accessory after the fact. But Wilson and Conant insisted that there was not a single speck of evidence, direct or circumstantial, in the confessions or in any testimony, that Otis Williams had actively participated in the murder of Joseph Felch. Indeed, the very confessions that were the core of the state's case contained evidence that Williams, rather than pursuing any deadly plots against his employer, was planning to leave him for good the following month.

After the closing arguments, Judge Stanton charged the jury on late Wednesday afternoon. He properly stressed the presumption of innocence, the concept of reasonable doubt, and that Otis Williams's failure to testify could not be held against him. Noting that Williams's attorneys had not stressed their client's mental state at the time of the murder, Stanton instructed the jurymen that if they believed that Williams had an active part in the murder and knew that Anna Felch was going to commit it, he was guilty of murder in the first degree. But if he did not have an active part but knew the facts, he might be found guilty of second-degree murder. After explaining the alternative verdicts of manslaughter or not guilty, Stanton sent the jury out at 6:05 PM.

They returned at 9:30 the next morning. Otis Williams was pale but calm as he was led into the courtroom, and he stood stolid and silent as the jury foreman pronounced him guilty of second-degree murder.

As he was led away to serve a mandatory life sentence in the Windsor Prison, Otis Williams probably knew that his accused accomplice had already delayed, if not denied, justice. The previous morning, Anna's lawyers had filed for a continuance until September. As alleged during Otis's trial, Anna was indeed pregnant. That continuance and further delays were forthcoming both before and after Anna gave birth to a daughter, Blanche Addie Felch, on November 14, 1916. Notwithstanding some ambiguity, the father listed on the birth certificate was the late Joseph Felch.

When Anna's trial finally got under way on June 18, 1917, the new mother demonstrated that she had employed her prolonged sojourn in the Orange County Jail profitably. She was becomingly arrayed in black widow's weeds, and her demeanor was calm and intelligent as jury selection got under way at 2 PM. Also noticeable to all spectators was the appealing presence of Anna's baby in the courtroom.

As with the Williams trial, the jury selection process for Anna's prosecution was less prolonged than anticipated. In an effort to recruit a relatively unbiased panel, the jury pool was drawn largely from the western side of Orange County. Examining nearly forty prospective jurors, the state used five of its peremptory challenges, the defense its entire prescribed six. Like the Williams jury, Anna's panel was composed largely of middle-aged farmers. Her counsel was a stellar legal battery, boasting the likes of Rooney M. Harvey,

Richard A. Hoar, Alland G. Fay, and Orange County clerk Hale K. Darling. Once again, the prosecution was led by Vermont attorney general Herbert Barber, this time assisted by the new Orange County state's attorney, John C. Sherburne. The presiding judge was Fred M. Butler.

It became immediately clear that Anna's trial would not be a reprise of the Williams prosecution. As soon as the opening statements were completed, it was announced that the jury would visit the scene of the crime. The next morning at 8:30, a fleet of automobiles conveyed the jurymen, Judge Butler, the trial lawyers, and Anna Felch to Waits River. They spent several hours there, examining the Williams cottage, the Felch home, and the sugarhouse. All seemed the worse for the neglect they had suffered during the fourteen-month interval, and lawyers Barber and Fay were available to answer any questions the jury members might have. By the time they completed the twenty-six-mile trip back to the Chelsea courthouse, it was time to dine, and the jury was then excused for the day.

The prosecutors surprised everyone the next morning by calling Otis Williams as their first witness. His direct testimony differed little from the confessions read at his own trial. Speaking calmly and carefully, he repeated the shabby narrative of how he became sexually entangled with Anna Felch during the fall of 1915. He recounted the events of the night of April 22, swearing that he had not realized Anna was going to shoot her husband when he accompanied her to the sugarhouse. The only major new detail in his story was his recollection that he had heard Anna and Joseph arguing about her pregnancy several weeks before Joe was killed and that Joe suspected that Otis was the father. Although pale from his year in prison, Williams made a good impression and could not be tripped up during Richard Hoar's vigorous cross-examination.

Frank S. Williams was the next witness, and he reprised the

details of his murder investigation and his dealings with Otis Williams. He added little to the case against Anna, but the defense pulled off a coup by immediately recalling him as a *defense* witness after he left the stand. Once again, he was interrogated about the manner in which he had solicited the Williams confessions. And once again, Frank Williams succeeded in proving the strict legality of his stratagems—but not before the defense had a field day portraying the prosecutors as manipulative, disingenuous bullies.

Josephine Pero and George Hight testified next, followed by Dr. William Rowland. Hight's testimony that Anna had seemed unmoved by her husband's death was balanced by Pero's recollection that Anna had wept as they walked to the sugarhouse on Easter morn. And the effect of Dr. Rowland's testimony about Anna's oblivious insistence that Joe had committed suicide was softened by Anna's quiet weeping throughout much of his testimony, an edifying and womanly spectacle.

The testimony of minor witnesses consumed much of the following two days. Mary Williams was the most pathetic witness, although her testimony added little to the record. Her chief new disclosure was that she had perjured herself during Otis's preliminary hearing after his arrest on April 26, 1916. She had then sworn that Otis had returned home to stay by 8 PM on the murder night. She now admitted that Otis had left home again at 9 PM and not returned until around 11 PM. More interestingly, Alfred Follansbee testified that he had attended a Halloween sociable in Waits River in 1915. He saw Anna Felch and Otis Williams there, and the two of them mentioned that they had walked the two miles from her home together to attend the event, at which neither her husband nor Otis's wife were present. Over the protests of Barber and Sherburne, much of Follansbee's testimony was excluded as irrelevant by Judge Butler.

The state now tried hard to show that the relations between Anna and Joseph had deteriorated after Otis Williams came to work for them. But all John Sherburne could elicit from F. Warren Currier was that Anna and Otis had been "talkative," hardly the stuff of which murder motives are composed. Florence Currier, a hired girl who had worked in the Felch household, told the jury that Anna had once remarked that Otis Williams "had pretty eyes and pretty hair." Sherburne eventually prompted Florence to recount an incident in which Anna had said that "Joe and Otis ought to swap wives." But on cross-examination, the defense forced Florence to admit that Anna was laughing when she made the suggestion.

When the state rested at 3:50 on Tuesday afternoon, June 26, Anna's lawyers immediately asked Judge Butler to remove the case from the jury and issue a directed verdict of not guilty on the ground that virtually the only evidence against Anna came from Otis Williams, a self-confessed perjurer. After Judge Butler refused, Anna's defense immediately called John Felch, the victim's father, to testify. He told the jury that as far as he knew, relations between Anna and his son had been good. John's generally positive portrait of his son's marriage was further amplified by the next witness, John's wife, who recalled how pleased she had been when her son married Anna Smith. Then came Fred Bagley, who testified that he had sat next to Anna at Joe's funeral and that she had cried and "took on badly." Anna's brother, Fred Smith, followed Bagley. Although in ill health and seemingly confused, Fred aided his sister by shifting the focus back to Otis Williams, especially his suspicious behavior in the aftermath of Joseph Felch's death. Fred recalled Otis saying on Easter Sunday morning, "I am just the same as in the electric chair." He also related an odd incident in his sister's kitchen on the following day. One of Otis's boots had fallen with a loud thump on the floor. When Mary Williams asked Otis if he weren't going to pick it up, he replied, "No, I don't want to kill anyone else."

The turning point of the trial came at 4:25 on Wednesday afternoon of the trial's second week, when Anna Felch took the stand in her own defense. As the spectators in the packed courtroom watched, she walked firmly to the stand, seated herself, and explained that she had been born in Topsham, lived there until she was twenty-six, and had married Joseph Felch in 1908. She was soon confronted with virtually every accusation Otis Williams had made in his two confessions and as a prosecution witness. She denied them all, never losing her composure or allowing John Sherburne to confuse her. She had to be especially careful during his blistering cross-examination, as Sherburne deliberately avoided asking her questions in chronological order, forcing her to be cautious in her testimony. No, she had never had sexual relations with Otis Williams. No, she had never gone to the barn with him alone. No, she had not gone to the sugarhouse on the night before Easter Sunday. No, she had not killed her husband. She was emphatic in repudiating everything Otis Williams had charged, and she wept appropriately when recounting the finding of her husband's body.

Anna was less forthcoming and decisive when queried about her behavior after Joe's murder. Confronted with statements she had made during the initial investigation, she repeatedly replied, "I don't know," "I don't remember," or "I couldn't tell." She was positive, however, that she had never, ever said to Frank Williams: "I have an idea that [Joseph] killed himself, and he wanted me to go to the sugarhouse, and I think if I had gone we would both have been dead instead of one."

After Anna completed her testimony on Friday morning, both sides called their rebuttal witnesses. The most significant of them was Mary Williams, who recalled that Anna had said to her after the murder, "Don't tell them that Otis was away from the house that night—if you do they will arrest him."

Sherburne began the closing arguments in the case on Friday afternoon. He disclaimed any animus against Anna Felch and relied on a dispassionate restatement of the circumstantial evidence and the testimony. The theory he presented to the jury was simply that Anna, alarmed by the perils arising from her suspicious pregnancy, had successfully plotted to kill her husband. Sherburne cited in support the testimony documenting illicit relations between Otis Williams and Anna and laid special stress on Anna's request that Josephine Pero sleep with her as evidence of an uneasy conscience. He concluded with an appeal to the jury's commonsense logic: If Anna had *not* engaged in illicit sexual relations with Otis Williams, then what possible motive could Williams have had for killing Joseph Felch, a crime for which he had been convicted?

Hale K. Darling's final plea was a direct response to Sherburne's question. Characterizing the Felch marriage as happy, he painted an unattractive picture of Otis Williams, asking with rhetorical sarcasm, "Why should that woman exchange something for nothing? Why should she exchange a man for a skunk?"

With the final arguments completed on Saturday morning, Judge Butler charged the jury, and they went out at 2 PM. They returned four hours later—with a verdict of not guilty. As the verdict was announced, Anna burst into tears and then sat down. A moment later, she recovered her composure and began shaking hands with her attorneys before she was taken back to jail, pending final arrangements for her release.

Anna's troubles were not over yet. The Felch murder had aroused the local citizenry to an unprecedented degree, and the prominence of the legal talent its two trials attracted was a telling index of its elevated legal and political profile. And even if one rejoiced in Anna's acquittal, the verdict left most of the concerned lawmen, attorneys, and citizenry unsatisfied. Writing two days after Anna's acquittal, a correspondent for the *Barre Daily Times* put the problems raised by the trial in a nutshell:

> One may search the criminal records of every court in Vermont and fail to find a capital crime that caused such a wave of revulsion to sweep over the district where the murder of Joseph Felch was perpetrated. If the trial of Otis Williams, now serving a life sentence at Windsor for the murder, and the more recent ordeal which the farmer's wife has undergone, established any one fact beyond the peradventure of a doubt it is the fact that Joseph Felch apparently was without an enemy in the world. What sinister motive lay back of the crime is not fully established, even though a jury in the summer of 1916 decreed that Williams should pay almost the supreme penalty for the murder.

Given such public perplexities about the case, it was hardly surprising that Barber and Sherburne subsequently decided to appeal the verdict to the Vermont Supreme Court.

Notwithstanding the appeal hanging over her head, Anna's life began to assume some shades of normalcy after she was released from jail on July 9. Her parents had stuck by her from the beginning, and mother-in-law Mrs. John Felch had promised that if Anna were acquitted, "she would take her." One does wonder, however, what the feelings of her relations were when Anna married Leander Dexter on September 30, 1917.

On November 7 the Vermont Supreme Court ruled on the state's appeal of Anna's verdict. Siding with Barber and Sherburne, the court ruled that Judge Butler had erred in both allowing and disallowing testimony. Specifically, as Justice George M. Powers explained in his opinion, Butler should not have excluded the testimony about Otis and Anna's behavior at the Waits River sociable; at the same time, he should not have allowed frivolous speculation about a phantom "three-fingered killer" to creep into the trial record. Rejecting the defense contention that the state's appeal amounted to double jeopardy, the court ordered that Anna stand trial again.

Anna's predicament was not as bad as it seemed. On April 7, 1919, her lawyers filed her answering plea in the Orange County Court. Stripped of its interminable and numbing legalese, it claimed that she had been already tried and found not guilty and should be discharged. It was so argued by her attorneys on June 3, and the court promptly ruled the "respondent discharged and let go without delay." For whatever unknown reasons—perhaps fearing another embarrassing acquittal—prosecutors Barber and Sherburne chose not to revive the murder charge against Anna.

And so ended the sugarhouse murder. Life in Waits River returned to normal, and Anna and her family settled anew into the obscurity of rural life. Whatever public doubts or guilty feelings left festering over the disparate fates of Otis Williams and Anna Felch were at least partially satisfied five years later when Governor Redfield Proctor granted Williams a parole, and he exited the Windsor Prison on December 29, 1924. Twenty-two years later, on October 16, 1946, Williams received a full pardon from Governor Mortimer Proctor.

But the puzzle of the sugarhouse murder remains. If Otis Williams killed Joseph Felch, why did he do it? Was Anna Felch implicated in her husband's murder—or did the infatuated farmhand commit the murder "on spec" in hopes of eliminating and eventually replacing Anna's husband? Anna Felch and Otis Williams are long gone, and so is Joseph Felch's ill-starred sugarhouse. But the question of this rural Vermont gothic whodunit remains to puzzle and disquiet.

CHAPTER 3

"500 CLEAN DOLLARS"

The 1902 Murder of Marcus Rogers

Mary Mabel Rogers's last seven minutes were probably the best, or at least the best behaved, of her life. When Sheriff Henry H. Peck and his deputies came for her at 1:06 PM, she arose and walked silently to Windsor Prison matron Sarah Durkee's parlor, where she listened for a few moments to Father Cornelius C. Delaney's final prayer. Walking calmly to her doom, she clutched the crucifix attached to a gold chain around her neck, a last gift from her half-sister Catherine. As she had promised, Mary then walked unaided and quietly to the scaffold, only blanching a shade paler as she caught sight of the fatal rope. Still silent, she mounted the oaken steps, carefully clutching the folds of her black dress so as not to step on it. According to her request, she was wearing a new pair of shoes.

A minute later Sheriff Peck, following the solemn, ghastly ritual prescribed by law, asked her if there was any reason why sentence of death should not be passed upon her. She made no answer, simply continuing to stare into space as if she had not heard him. He repeated the question. Still no answer, and it seemed to the forty spectators present as if she were unaware of his query. As Deputy Sheriffs Thomas and McDermott stepped forward to pinion her arms and ankles, she removed her eyeglasses. Handing them to one of the deputies, she said, "These are for my sister. Please see that she gets them."

Mary's hands and ankles were securely tied with rope. Deputy Sheriff Romaine Spafford placed the traditional black cowl over her head. He then said to her, "I now execute the sentence of the law, and may God have mercy on your soul." She nodded and repeated the words, almost inaudibly, "May God have mercy on my soul." A second later Deputy Sheriff Angus McAuley pressed his foot on the wooden trigger, and Mary Rogers hurtled downward, the last woman ever to be executed by hanging in Vermont, on December 8, 1905. How had this seemingly stoic young woman come to this ignoble end?

———

Depending on one's view, the Mary Mabel Rogers saga might be suitable fare for either an antique penny dreadful or a Eugene O'Neill play—a tritely rural gothic insurance murder or a true-life Vermont summer-stock version of *Desire Under the Elms*. It all depends, most probably, on one's estimate of Mary herself. Was she a coldly calculating, if careless and promiscuous, virago who plotted her husband's demise for a mere $500 insurance policy and the lure of a new sexual playmate? Or was she just a mentally and spiritually stunted near-moron with no real sense of right or wrong, a pitiful but inevitable product of her genes and environment?

Whatever Mary's true nature, surely Marcus Merritt Rogers might have chosen a more compatible spouse. Both originally from the Hoosick Falls, New York, area, Mary and Marcus met sometime in the late 1890s, probably in upstate New York. Although the subsequent opinion of his kith and kin was that Marcus was no mental giant, he still should have known better. Only fifteen years old when she married the twenty-seven-year-old Marcus in 1898, Mary, by all accounts, was a vicious, ignorant hellion well before they plighted their troubled troth. Born out of wedlock to a criminal father and a mentally subnormal mother on March 9, 1883, Mary became an orphan six months later and was raised by Johanna Callahan. An immature, restless youth who hungered for excitement, Mary continually tormented the more conventional, retiring Marcus with incessant material demands and by roaming from their farmhouse home of an evening. During the four years of their troubled marriage they lived in Hoosick Falls and Walloomsac, New York, and in nearby Bennington and Shaftsbury. Clearly Mary wasn't cut out to be a farmer's wife, and she punctuated their union with frequent and increasingly lengthy absences. It didn't help that chronic poverty dogged their marriage from the beginning.

Worse was to come. Mary had a baby in the spring of 1901, while they were living in Shaftsbury. In the middle of a subsequent September day, she came running to a neighbor's house, crying that she had accidentally dropped her baby at home. When the neighbor returned with Mary, they found the infant dying of a fractured skull. There was no inquest; unexplained infant deaths were not uncommon in that era, and Mary was the only witness to the tragedy. But suspicion was rife among Marcus Rogers's blood relations that Mary had deliberately killed her infant. Such dark misgivings waxed exponentially several months later when Marcus became violently, dangerously ill after drinking tea prepared for him by Mary. Shortly after that incident Mary moved out of the house. But Marcus would hear no ill word of his teenaged wife. Whatever Mary's provocations, Marcus continued to cling to the hope that he could somehow patch up their foundering marriage.

By the spring of 1902, however, there was little to cling to. Owing in part to their enduring poverty, Marcus was working as a mere day laborer on his brother William's farm in Hoosick Falls. During Mary's infrequent visits there and Marcus's occasional pilgrimages to see her in Bennington, he would plead with her to come back to him and live as a normal couple. But Mary always refused, citing their poverty and her relatively comfortable circumstances in Bennington.

Most witnesses to Mary's Bennington sojourn would probably have used a harsher term than "comfortable" to describe her lifestyle. In the spring of 1902 she was living at the Spaulding rooming house on East Main Street. Also in residence there was one Estella ("Stella") Bates, a young woman of Mary's age, and of like ephemeral loyalties and dubious chastity. Both girls had a taste for such irregular nightlife as Bennington afforded, and it seems any number of young men frolicked with them during their residence at the Spaulding house and elsewhere. Eventually, in June 1902, Mary met two men there who would fatally change her life.

One was twenty-one-year-old Morris Knapp, then living with his family on Birch Street. When not toiling as a manual laborer, Morris fulfilled his occasional obligations as a member of the Vermont National Guard. Both commitments left him with ample leisure, and he was more than happy to cultivate the acquaintance of such accessible ladies as Mary and Stella. Several weeks after meeting him, Mary moved out of the Spaulding house to board at the home of Emmett and Laura Perham on Beech Street. Also in residence there were the Perham sons, Levi, twenty-eight, and Leon, eighteen. A month later, in July, the Perham family relocated to a home on Safford Street. With them went Mary and her new paramour Morris Knapp. Soon after, Mary was enjoying sexual relations with Knapp and both of the Perham brothers.

Knapp would later claim that Mary told him from the start that she was a single woman. His assertion was probably true. As their relationship ripened and the subject of Marcus Rogers eventually came up, Mary explained him away by insisting he was her brother. Indeed, she told Knapp that she and Leon had recently attended Marcus's wedding in Hoosick Falls. Whether Morris believed that Mary was single, however, is probably irrelevant. Morris Knapp wasn't the kind of man to fret about such formalities; he was having a very good time with Mary on her rudimentary bed—a mattress and box springs—during those long summer nights in her second-floor front bedroom on Safford Street, and there is no evidence that he ever took his relations with Mary Rogers very seriously.

Unfortunately for Marcus Rogers, Leon Perham took *his* relations with Mary *very* seriously. By the middle of that July he was sexually besotted with her. By all accounts, Leon, like Marcus Rogers, was not a very shrewd person, and it was the work of only several weeks for Mary to bend him to the needs of her dread purpose. That purpose, which she unfolded to him over early August pillow talk, was to kill her husband.

Leon was not Mary's first choice. She had been forming her plans for some time, and on Sunday, August 10, she tried to recruit Leon's older brother Levi to her plot. While sitting with him and Stella Bates on a stone wall at Main and Bradford Streets, Mary asked him to help her kill her husband. She promised Levi she would pay him "500 clean dollars" from the proceeds of Marcus's life insurance policy. Levi, who had been drinking, initially agreed to the proposal. But after sober second thought, he backed out. Strangely—or perhaps not so strangely in that peculiar Perham family—he did not inform the Bennington police authorities about Mary's murderous scheme. He did tell his mother, Laura, but both of them apparently decided that it was just idle talk.

It wasn't idle talk to the sexually infatuated Leon, whom Mary now more successfully approached with the same scheme. He readily agreed, and all was soon in readiness for committing the murder on the night of Tuesday, August 12. The only thing wanting was the victim.

He duly appeared on the afternoon of the twelfth. After meeting Mary at the Spaulding house at her invitation, Marcus sauntered with her through the Bennington streets, earnestly pleading with her to come and live with him at his brother's farm. They parted at about 6 PM. Mary's version of their parting was that when she refused to return with him, Marcus became hysterical, pulled out a book containing the record of his insurance payments, and hurled it into her lap, exclaiming that she should take it, as she would "never look on his living face again."

Whatever Mary's later lies, it is an established fact that Marcus showed up an hour later at the Bennington home of his cousins, Mabel and Myrtle Phillipott. To them he said nothing of any recent trouble with his wife, and he even showed them his insurance book. After eating supper with the Phillipotts, Marcus departed at about 8 PM. He said he was going to meet his Mary, and left his umbrella and a medicine bottle behind him—indications he intended to return there before he left Bennington. An hour later, Marcus dropped in on Frank Shaw, another relative, at his home on Congress Street. Marcus left there about 10 PM and was never seen alive again by anyone, except his murderers.

The Chicago columnist Mike Royko once commented on the moronic behavior often exhibited by those who hire killers to eliminate their erstwhile loved ones. When one hires a plumber, for instance, one usually insists, or at least has good reason to assume, that said plumber has some expertise at plumbing. So, too, with the usual credentials or bona fides expected of, say, a schoolteacher or an automobile mechanic. But it is a perverse truth that when people solicit hired killers, they almost invariably enlist incompetent amateurs, more often than not someone like the janitor of their apartment building, a bumbling novice possessing only a rudimentary education and no experience at successful homicide.

So, too, was it with Mrs. Rogers's willing but not too wise tool, Leon Perham. Although he had known Mary only a few weeks, Leon, with no experience in the murder-for-hire line, agreed to help kill her husband. More astonishing still, he was persuaded to do so—Mary's previous sexual favors and the lure of the $500 notwithstanding—on the clear understanding that Mary's chief motive for murder was her belief that Morris Knapp—not Leon—would marry her once her current husband was eliminated.

Whatever his confused reasoning on the matter, Leon was sleeping when Mary came to his room at the Perham house at 9:30 PM on August 12. She woke him up, and after they discussed their plans she said, "Are you ready?" Leon assented—and immediately fell back to sleep. Mary woke him up again at about 11 PM. Leon got dressed and they silently tiptoed down the back stairs of the house to the porch in their stocking feet. There, they put on their shoes, tied the door shut with a piece of rope, and walked out into the night.

It didn't take long to get to the murder scene. They walked up Safford Street, turned onto County Street, then followed Grove Street all the way to a somewhat wooded area by the Walloomsac River known as Morgan's Grove. It was a warm night, dark and cloudy.

Mary and Leon had been waiting for about half an hour when Marcus Rogers showed up. Marcus didn't seem to find Leon's presence there odd, and they sat on a stone wall chatting for a few minutes. Then Mary suggested that they sit on the ground. Marcus lay there for several minutes, his head in Mary's lap, while she talked to him in an uncharacteristically solicitous way about his health and work.

The critical moment came at about 11:30 PM. Mary said to Marcus, "Stella Bates did some tricks today with a rope. Let me show them to you. Leon, give me that rope." Taking the rope that Leon had brought, Mary turned to Marcus and said, "Give me your hands." She tied his hands behind him and defied him to escape from her cunning knot. She carefully disguised her surprised chagrin when he did so immediately. Turning to Leon, she said, "*You* take the rope and tie it."

As soon as Leon tied the knot, Mrs. Rogers grabbed Marcus's head and shoved a bottle of chloroform under his nose. Even as Marcus tried to holler "Stop!" Mary screamed to Leon, "Hold his legs! Hold his legs!" It took twenty minutes for Marcus to die, as Mary grimly held the bottle to his nose and Leon hung on to his desperately thrashing legs. Finally Marcus stopped moving, and Leon and Mary collapsed in frantic exhaustion.

Leon was beside himself with panic, but Mary was equal to the awful moment. "You've got to take the jackknife out and cut the rope and get it off his hands," she dictated. "Then you take him and roll him into the river and cover him up so that nobody can see his clothes." Before the body splashed into the Walloomsac, however, Mary had the presence of mind to rifle Marcus's pockets and retrieve his insurance payment book. Then she picked up Marcus's hat, which he had left lying on the ground by his coat. After nailing it to a nearby tree, she pinned a "suicide" note to it, which she had carefully composed several hours before. It read:

Blame no one as I have at last put an end to my miseberl life as my wife nows I have every threatened it, every nows I have not enything or no body to live for no one can blame me and so blame no one as my last request. [Signed] Marcus Rogers

P. s. May i ope you will be happy

The two killers then returned to the Perham home, removed their shoes, and tiptoed back up the stairs to Mary's room.

Whatever talents Mary Rogers possessed, she apparently was not blessed with beginner's luck, at least regarding the homicide trade. Pursuing her flimsy script that Marcus had committed suicide, she walked downtown the next morning and sought out Bennington County sheriff John Nash. Appearing tearfully distraught, she told him that she had quarreled with her husband the day before. Now Marcus was missing, she whimpered, and she feared he had done away with himself.

Later that morning Mary dropped in on the Phillipott sisters. Flourishing Marcus's insurance book, she repeated her fiction about their Tuesday afternoon quarrel and her fears that Marcus had killed himself. "I feel that something may have happened to Marcus," she hinted darkly. "I feel he may have drowned himself."

The Phillipott sisters must have realized Mary was lying. They had both seen the insurance book in Marcus's possession the night before. And Mary's particular observation, apropos of nothing, that his leaving his umbrella and medicine bottle behind at their house indicated that he never intended to come back seemed peculiar to them, as they had not mentioned them, and Mary could not have seen those items, given her vantage point when she called at the house that morning. Later that afternoon she encountered Morris Knapp, who had just returned from his annual muster with Company K of the Vermont National Guard at Fort Ethan Allen in

Essex Junction. To him she repeated her misgivings about Marcus and, no doubt, repeated her oft-expressed wish that they might soon be joined in holy wedlock.

Meanwhile, things weren't going as planned with the suicide scenario. Mary's expectation had been that the suicide note and her husband's corpse would be discovered immediately. A man named John Sanborn did notice Marcus's hat on Wednesday morning but did not investigate it further. Others, too, apparently saw it, but it wasn't until Wednesday evening that Bennington resident E. Payson Hathaway spied the hat with a note pinned to it—and he didn't get around to taking it down and reading the note until the next morning. He then took the note and hat to storekeeper Samuel Jewett, and the two men subsequently found the corpse in the river about 9 AM, lying facedown in two feet of water. County sheriff Nash and his deputy Fred Godfrey were summoned, and they pulled the body out of the river. After letting the corpse dry out a little, they took it to the undertaking parlor of James E. Walbridge. A watch and purse in the dead man's pockets identified the body as that of Marcus Rogers, and his wife was quickly notified. Mary's landlady, Laura Perham, agreed to allow the body to be brought into her house for the obsequies after Mary promised her a cut from her husband's $500 insurance policy. It was only then, Mrs. Perham later insisted, that she learned that her promiscuous boarder was married.

Mrs. Perham was just beginning to learn about the real Mary Rogers. The following morning Mary came down from her room and burned a large packet of papers in the kitchen stove. She also concealed her ink and writing paper, something she had not hitherto done. She then paid a visit downtown to James Reilly, the agent for the Metropolitan Life Insurance Company. Brandishing her husband's policy and payment book, Mary asked if the policy was in force and whether she was the beneficiary. She was pleased when Reilly replied yes to both queries. She was less gratified, however, when Reilly informed her that payment would have to await the verdict of the coroner's inquest on her husband's death, scheduled for that very afternoon.

Ever ready to improvise, Mary returned to the Perham residence. She informed Laura and Levi that the three of them were wanted at the inquest that afternoon. She then told them exactly what she wanted them to say there, especially emphasizing the notion that Marcus Rogers must have committed suicide. It is unknown what response Laura and Levi made to her demands, but Laura Perham would later insist that when Mary left the room, she turned to her son and piously entreated him to tell only the truth.

The coroner's inquest began promptly at 2 PM, presided over by justice of the peace John D. Shurtleff. The initial testimony was inconclusive and puzzling. Several persons testified to the circumstances surrounding the discovery of the body, and then physicians Emmett Daley and H. J. Potter presented the mystifying results of their just-completed autopsy. Despite the initial presumption that Marcus Rogers had drowned himself, there was no water in the lungs of the corpse. And although there was an ugly bruise over one eye, it was not considered sufficient to have caused death. Both doctors confessed themselves unable to state the cause of death.

The Rogers case began to open up later that afternoon with the testimony of Levi Perham. Calmly, he testified about Mary soliciting him to help kill her husband in Hoosick Falls. The plan, he said, was to trick Marcus into physically exhausting himself by challenging him to a skip-rope contest. Then Mary would fall on the panting Marcus with chloroform, while Levi held his legs.

People in small towns tend to be known quantities to their neighbors. It had been obvious to Bennington lawmen where the

Rogers case was heading even before the inquest opened, and as Levi commenced his testimony, United States marshal Emory S. Harris drew an obviously anxious Leon Perham aside and began talking to him in a kindly but firm manner. It probably took little persuasion to make Leon open up, as he was already almost visibly writhing in paroxysms of remorse. So when he followed his brother on the stand, he immediately blurted out a complete confession. As he was led away, Mrs. Rogers took the stand. Carefully sequestered during Leon's testimony and unaware that he had told all, she proceeded to hopelessly implicate herself in a damning thicket of lies. After more testimony the following day, Leon Perham led lawmen to his room at his parents' home, where he turned over the rope and the chloroform used in the murder. On Saturday night, August 16, Mary Rogers, Stella Bates, and Leon Perham were arraigned on first-degree murder charges before Justice Shurtleff. All three of them knew that the penalty for first-degree murder was hanging. They all pleaded not guilty.

After the three accused were duly indicted by a Bennington grand jury in June 1903, plans went forward for what were expected to be three trials of unprecedented sensationalism. The original plan was to try Leon Perham first, but Mrs. Rogers earned that honor after Bennington authorities realized that using Leon as a cooperative witness against her might ultimately save them the expense of two potentially lengthy trials.

Almost sixteen months after Marcus Rogers was murdered, the trial of Mary Rogers finally got under way on the morning of Wednesday, December 9, 1903. With Common Pleas Court judge John H. Watson presiding, the state's case was prosecuted by Orion ("Olin") M. Barber and Jacob J. Shakshober. Defending Mary Rogers were Daniel A. Guiltinan and Frank C. Archibald. From a jury pool of fifty-eight men, twelve jurors were finally seated by the following morning. The initial crowd of spectators in the courtroom was large, if not quite as large as predicted. Judge Watson soon made his strict standards of courtroom decorum clear by ejecting two unruly spectators even before jury selection was completed.

Judge Watson was an impartial, responsible jurist, and he saw to it that Mary Rogers received a fair trial with due respect to the law. Whether Mary's defense was inadequate, as she would later complain, is a thornier question. Surely, Guiltinan and Archibald had little to work with and a very exasperating client. The chain of circumstantial evidence against Mary was substantial and unbroken, and she lacked an alibi witness to counter any particular of the state's murder narrative. Mary apparently didn't wish to testify in her own behalf, and her attorneys doubtless considered any such appearance inimical. And while her silence, as Judge Watson cautioned the jury, could not be held against her, there is little doubt that her courtroom demeanor and behavior hurt her with the jury, the public, and the press. Unwilling or unable to play to the era's sentimental stereotypes about woman as emotional creatures, Mary maintained throughout her trial an apparently stolid, unblinking indifference that damned her to all as an unfeeling, indeed *unfemale,* monster. Although she did sob visibly during prosecutor Shakshober's final argument, most courtroom reporters would have heartily echoed Orion Barber's characterization of her courtroom demeanor as exhibiting "a brazen and callous effrontery that was astounding." Still, most observers allowed that Mary was an attractive woman: tall, well built, with flashing black eyes and long, raven-black hair.

The state's case was a model of carefully marshaled details, eyewitness testimony, and expert witnesses. After several witnesses testified about the discovery of Marcus Rogers's body and the purported suicide note, Leon Perham was called to the stand. His testimony, as the *Rutland Herald* termed it the following day, was "not especially adapted for a drawing room conversation." After Judge Watson overruled defense objections to allowing his testimony, Leon poured out his tawdry tale in a halting, sometimes incoherent, and often confused fashion. Seemingly dazed, he was at times clearly unable to understand prosecutor Barber's questions. As one reporter put it, "It has always been claimed that the young man was not mentally balanced, and his appearance on the witness stand would indicate the truth of those statements." For all that, however, the mundanely specific detail of Leon's story and his obvious remorse were tremendously persuasive to most of his audience. He told of his sexual involvement with Mrs. Rogers, her plea that he help murder her husband, and the events of the night of August 12. And despite the defense lawyers' partially successful attempts to confuse him in cross-examination, Leon's evidence against Mrs. Rogers was all the more convincing because the jury knew that he was also knowingly incriminating himself.

The medical testimony presented did not aid Mrs. Rogers's defense. Drs. Daley and Potter, who had conducted the postmortem, insisted that Rogers's death could not have been caused by the blow over his eye and was consistent with "the forcible application of chloroform." Dr. Daley's testimony about Mrs. Rogers herself was more damning than the medical facts. Mrs. Rogers, Daley testified, had actually been present during the dissection of her husband's corpse. Not only had she not shied away from witnessing the grisly procedure, Daley stated, but she had repeatedly asked if there was any poison found in Marcus's organs. She appeared "cool and unexcited," Daley continued, and seemed most intent on declaiming an account of her Tuesday afternoon quarrel with her husband. Two medical experts followed with testimony about the analysis of the corpse's organs, and it was noted disapprovingly by courtroom spectators that Mrs. Rogers seemed entirely unfazed by the presence of those organs in a jar just several feet away from her.

After various witnesses testified about the toxicity of the Rogerses' marriage, Morris Knapp took the stand. Spectators hoping for the squalid details of his relationship with Mrs. Rogers were initially disappointed when Judge Watson advised Knapp that he could not be forced to incriminate himself with regard to his adulterous relationship with her. Thereafter, Knapp primly answered questions about their sexual involvement with the statement, "I do not care to answer, unless I am compelled to it." Much to his dismay, he subsequently *was* compelled to it, after Judge Watson ruled that Knapp had to answer questions about his relations with Mrs. Rogers *after* Mr. Rogers's death occurred, when such relations would no longer have constituted criminal adultery. Reluctantly, Knapp admitted spending the night after Marcus's death fornicating with Mary in her second-floor bedroom at the Perham house. There were limits, however, Knapp insisted, to his callousness. After Marcus's death and Mrs. Rogers's apparent guilt were discovered on Thursday, Knapp testified, Mrs. Rogers had sent him a note, begging him to come to her. "Perham has let it all out," she wrote. "Come and comfort me quick." As he now testified, Knapp had righteously refused to comfort her on that occasion, in part because he was disquieted by the knowledge that Marcus's corpse was lying in the parlor below her bedroom. Morris's brother Henry Knapp then testified that Mary had sent a man to fetch Knapp later that same evening. Henry had sent word back to Mary that "with a dead husband at home she ought to be doing something else besides chasing up other men."

Levi Perham followed Knapp on the stand, telling the jury without any apparent embarrassment how Mary had tried to recruit him first as her co-murderer. Then came Laura Perham and the Phillipott sisters, whose testimony limned Mary's clumsy efforts to fabricate the narrative of her husband's suicide. It only remained for several handwriting experts to thoroughly demolish Mary's amateurish "suicide" note. W. H. Roberts noted that the handwriting on the note perfectly matched samples of Mary's known handwriting seized in her room. Moreover, the purported suicide note contained characteristic misspellings and peculiarities of letter formation found frequently in Mary's known handwriting samples but never in documents proved to be in Marcus's hand. In both the suicide note and in her other writings, for example, Mary misspelled "any" as "eny." The signer of the note had also joined the "R" and the "o" in "Rogers," something Marcus had never done in signing his name. Two other handwriting experts agreed with Roberts, and all of them concluded that the note was written in a "disguised or feigned" hand, that hand being the nearly illiterate one of Mary Rogers.

Neither Archibald nor Guiltinan was able to make a dent in the state's overwhelming evidence, despite their sometimes vigorous cross-examination of witnesses. When the state finally rested its case at 4:23 PM on Friday, December 18, the courtroom audience looked forward to the defense counterattack the next morning. Surely, some sturdy counter-testimony was to be put forward, despite the rumor that not a single witness for the defense had been subpoenaed.

After conferring with Judge Watson and the prosecutors at the opening of court the next day, Archibald and Guiltinan rested their client's case without calling a single witness. Although Mrs. Rogers later criticized the handling of her case, the decision of her lawyers to rely on the prosecution's evidence was apparently made with her compliance. It was said that it was the first time in Vermont history that a murder defendant had allowed her case to rest solely on the prosecution's evidence.

Prosecutor Shakshober opened his final argument with a calm summary of the overwhelming evidence against Mary. He recalled the vivid details of Leon Perham's story, the testimony of the Phillipott sisters, and the interesting histories of Marcus Rogers's insurance payment book and "suicide note." An honest review of the evidence by the jury, Shakshober concluded, could leave no reasonable doubt that Mary had plotted and executed her husband's death with premeditation and malice aforethought.

Defender Guiltinan's final argument surprised many trial observers. Rather than dealing with the evidence, he mounted a fullbore character assassination of Morris Knapp. It was Knapp—whom Mary Rogers desired to marry—who probably had the greatest motive for wanting Marcus Rogers dead, Guiltinan insisted. Was it not plausible, he continued, that the weak-minded Leon Perham had decided to do his friend Morris a "favor" by bumping off the human obstacle to his unfettered access to Mary? Repeatedly denouncing Knapp as the "lowest kind of scoundrel," Guiltinan also attacked Leon Perham's testimony, stating his belief that "no jury would find a woman guilty of murder upon the testimony of a weak-minded, lovesick youth." Guiltinan may have gone a bit too far in straining the credulity of the jury, however, when he blandly characterized the relations between Marcus and Mary as "as pleasant as those between the majority of married people." The evidence of the murder aside, quite a number of the trial witnesses had testified to the sorry state of the Rogerses' marriage.

The trial recessed early at noon on Saturday, December 19, postponing the final two closing arguments until Monday afternoon. This was done lest the case go to the jury on the weekend before Christmas—the fear being that Mary's jury might be in an injudicious hurry to reach a verdict before the weekend passed. When court reopened on Monday, Archibald's final defense plea echoed Guiltinan's excoriation of "self-confessed criminal" Morris Knapp and Leon Perham's dubious testimony. Archibald also attempted to introduce some minor quibbling about the testimony of the handwriting experts but, like his co-counsel, prudently steered clear of most of the circumstantial evidence. His final argument to the jury was a measure of his client's desperate plight. Employing a counterintuitive line of reasoning, Archibald actually asserted that if his client were really the calculating, cold-blooded mastermind killer the state had portrayed, she would never have left so much incriminating evidence lying around in the wake of the murder.

Orion Barber closed for the state. Focusing on a painstaking narrative of Marcus Rogers's movements from the time he arrived in Bennington on the afternoon of August 12 until his corpse was fished out of the Walloomsac River at 9 AM on August 14, Barber carefully charted the inconsistencies between Mary's fictional narrative of his demise and the actual timeline recreated by eyewitness testimony and circumstantial evidence. He then took up Archibald's argument that such a plethora of incriminating evidence would never have been left behind by a criminal mastermind. Barber reminded the jury that "no crime has ever been committed which, in looking back over it, did not show at least one defect which pointed out the criminal to all the world." "Gentleman of the jury—she forgot," intoned Barber as he began his litany of Mary's many mistakes. He continued with a recitation of each and every error in her machinations, each time concluding with the words, "She forgot." Again and again, Barber repeated the phrase, until, as one observer wrote, "it took on a tone of almost Edgar Allan Poe." There was no reasonable doubt, Barber finished, that Mary Rogers had killed her husband and should be convicted of first-degree murder.

Judge Watson's charge to the jury was the usual explication of what constituted premeditation and malice. He also emphasized Mary's right to a presumption of innocence until proven guilty by the evidence. Watson also addressed the question of what value the jury should give Leon Perham's evidence, instructing them that they themselves must decide what weight to give it, but that it could not be ignored. Watson ended his charge with an explanation of what constituted reasonable doubt, and the Rogers jury went out at 6:00 on the evening of Monday, December 21, 1903.

The jury returned when court reopened at 9:00 the next morning. Mrs. Rogers arrived on the hour and exhibited her usual impassive demeanor. As one hostile press observer put it, she "walked steadily and met the gaze of the crowd without flinching and had the point at issue been less vital it would have appeared as though she enjoyed the sensation she was creating."

There was a hush in the courtroom as clerk of courts Harry T. Cushman asked the jury to stand. Cushman then said, "Gentlemen of the jury, what have you for a verdict?"

"Guilty of murder in the first degree," replied jury foreman Oscar R. Chase.

A reporter for the *Bennington Banner* recorded his impressions of the defendant as the verdict was delivered: "Mrs. Rogers, on whose face had been the trace of a smile when the jury was told to stand up, resumed her normal expression of brutal don't care and after hesitating a moment, sat down." Judge Watson then deferred the sentencing to December 29. It would later be disclosed that the jury had taken an informal ballot immediately after they went out at 6 PM the previous day. It had been a unanimous vote for a first-degree murder verdict, and they had merely ratified that decision with a formal vote in the morning.

Popular opinion was that Leon Perham expected lenient treatment from the judicial system, especially in light of his complete cooperation in the prosecution of Mary Rogers. That same afternoon, he appeared before Judge Watson and pleaded guilty to second-degree murder. Leon may or may not have known that the only legal penalty for that crime in Vermont was life imprisonment. About an hour later, the charges against Stella Bates were dropped, and she was ordered released from the Bennington County Jail. It had apparently been decided some time before Mary's trial that it was hardly worth prosecuting Miss Bates. Although it was likely that she had known of the murder plot in advance and had procured the fatal chloroform from Ayre's drugstore in Hoosick Falls, it might be difficult to hang a first-degree murder rap on her using unreliable witnesses like Morris Knapp and the Perham brothers. It was reported that the Rogers jury would dearly have loved to have a crack at Morris Knapp, whom they considered a culpable cad.

Mary Rogers's celebrated calm deserted her as the verdict against her began to sink in. She began sobbing and moaning when she returned to her cell, and deteriorated into complete hysteria when she discovered that her pal Stella was departing. Stella, for her part, showed her continuing regard for Mary by helping the matron remove from her such temptations to suicide as her steel corset and hairpins. That same night, Stella, who could scarcely believe her good fortune after sixteen months in jail, happily fled Bennington on a train to New York.

Mary's disposition didn't improve after her sentencing on December 29. That morning a packed courtroom watched as she and Leon were led in together for sentencing. When Mary rose to her feet, Judge Watson asked her if there was any reason why the sentence of the court should not be pronounced. Raising one hand, then the other to her forehead, Mary croaked out in a barely audible voice, "I'm not guilty!"

Judge Watson then replied, "The sentence of this court is that you, the said Mary M. Rogers, on the first Friday of February, 1905, between the hours of one and two o'clock of the afternoon of said day, within the walls or enclosed yard of the State prison at Windsor, in the County of Windsor, be hanged by the neck until dead. And may God have mercy on your soul."

Following the provisions of Vermont's capital punishment law, Watson also sentenced Mary to three months' solitary confinement preceding her execution. Although every eye in the room was focused on her, Mary showed no emotion as her death sentence was pronounced, keeping her eyes fixed on the west wall window of the courtroom.

Then it was Leon's turn. He began to visibly tear up as Watson sentenced him to life in prison at hard labor. But he managed to get hold of himself and stared out of a nearby window until he mastered his feelings. It was noticed that the courtroom spectators seemed surprised at the severity of both sentences. They shouldn't have been: Vermont law left no discretion to the judge to mitigate the penalties imposed on Mary and Leon.

During the weeks and months that followed, Mary reverted to her impassive self. She soon abandoned her outright denials that she had killed her husband, switching to a strategy that implicated unnamed others and sanitized her motivation. Before leaving for the prison in Windsor, she granted a final interview to a reporter from the *Bennington Banner*. Asked whether she had killed Marcus, she hedged, insisting she "didn't mean to kill him." Painting herself as the real victim, she complained that, if only the "truth" were known, "the one who laid the plans and schemed the most in the matter would not now be walking the streets a free man. [But] I have been convicted and am doing all the suffering and I will not try to get anybody else in trouble as they tried to me. I wish no harm to anybody." Told of Morris Knapp's recent marriage, she began to sound more like her old venomous self: "To think of all I did for him only to have him get up on the stand and lie about me to save his own skin. . . . Morris Knapp's testimony was all lies. He knew I was a married woman the first time he saw me and teased me into things I never thought of until he suggested them."

Embroidering her self-portrait of calumniated virtue, she continued her indictment of her late associates: "Leon Perham told a pack of lies. Morris Knapp lied, the Phillipotts lied and if I should tell the truth everybody should say I was lying, too. The truth has not been told. If it should be it would open the people's eyes in Bennington and I should not be going to Windsor with a rope hanging over me."

Queried one last time as to whether she had killed Marcus, she replied, "I am convicted of killing him, and whatever I may say now would do me no good."

Considering the passivity of her original criminal defense, the ensuing legal struggle for Mary Rogers's life was a hard-fought, lengthy contest. Mary's first and best hope was the Vermont State Legislature. Under Vermont law, only the legislature—not the governor—then had the power to commute her death sentence. And her initial odds of such a commutation must have looked favorable. The state of Vermont had not executed anyone since 1891, when Sylvester Bell of Fairfax was hanged for the murder of his wife. At least eight condemned murderers had been spared by legislative commutation since then, and Mary's chances were even better, as she was a woman. Only one woman had ever been executed in Vermont, poisoner Emeline Meaker of Waterbury on March 30, 1883, so it must have seemed unlikely that Mary Rogers would become the second. What's more, her legal defenders had more than a year to save her life, as Vermont law prescribed at least one legislative session intervene between her sentencing and her execution.

Mary wasn't the only one surprised by the ultimate turn of events. Things began promisingly enough with the introduction of two bills in the legislature in October 1904. The first was to abolish capital punishment in Vermont; the second to commute Mary's sentence. As it happened, the latter was introduced by the newly elected representative from Manchester, her defense lawyer Frank Archibald. The first setback came, however, on November 16, 1904, when the Vermont House of Representatives turned down the bill to abolish capital punishment by a vote of 153 to 83. Efforts now turned to the floor fight over the bill containing Mary's commutation. Mary's fight for mercy was led by the Reverend D. J. O'Sullivan, a Catholic priest from St. Albans. His plea was just as stoutly opposed by the Reverend D. L. Hilliard, a Congregational minister from Cabot, who passionately demanded Mary's blood: "Gentleman, you dare not vote to commute this woman's sentence! You dare not do it! I swear to you, gentlemen, before my God, if she was my own sister, I would vote to hang her!"

Even a direct appeal to the legislators by Mary's mother, Johanna Callahan, was of no avail. In an emotional speech, Mrs. Callahan blamed Mary's conviction on the fact that Bennington was full of Marcus's relatives. The final vote on the bill to commute Mary's death sentence failed, 139 to 91. It was said that Frank Archibald cried like a child as the vote was tallied. He had done his utmost, telling his fellow legislators that Mary was no more than a "great animal," with "no perception of right and wrong." The legislators next turned down a joint resolution asking Governor Charles J. Bell to appoint a panel with a view to determining Mary's sanity and delaying her execution until at least 1906. After the resolution was rejected, Mary's partisans asked Governor Bell to convene a special session of the legislature for another try at commutation. But Bell refused, stating his views on Mary Rogers unequivocally: "I shall never interfere to save the woman. The people of Vermont think she should be hanged, and I am going to see that the sentence is carried out. No person ever deserved hanging more than she."

Rebuffed repeatedly by the legislature and the executive, Mary's partisans turned their efforts to the appeals process. Given Judge Watson's careful handling of the trial, Mary's attorneys had waived their legal exceptions, and they had not even filed a motion for a new trial after her original conviction. So the legal drive to save Mary, based on alleged new evidence, began with an appeal to the Vermont Supreme Court. On February 1, 1905, two days before Mary's scheduled execution, Governor Bell held a hearing in Montpelier for parties interested in saving Mary Rogers's life. After listening to their arguments and perusing affidavits offering evidence of Mary's insanity as justification for a new trial, Bell reprieved Mary until June 2, so that her appeal could be forwarded to the Vermont Supreme Court.

Mary's appeal to the high court was based mainly on new affidavits collected by her lawyers. The most important of them contained the testimony of Dr. Leroy D. MacWayne of Hoosick Falls. MacWayne swore under oath that he had been approached by Marcus Rogers on August 7, 1902. Rogers was concerned about his wife's health, and his visit triggered a subsequent visit by Mary to MacWayne's office on Sunday, August 10, 1902. According to MacWayne, a distraught Mary had demanded that he provide her with "dangerous drugs"—abortifacients. MacWayne had refused, and Mary had become violent and threatened his life. MacWayne had then examined Mary, confirmed she was pregnant, and diagnosed her as suffering from "puerperal insanity," triggered by her "delicate condition." Other affidavits supported the claims of Mary's partisans that she and her whole family were subnormal in intelligence and behavior.

Mary's legal appeal also contained an affidavit from Windsor Prison superintendent Wilson S. Lovell. Lovell's testimony was that he had been present at an interview between Leon Perham and attorney E. B. Flynn on January 31, 1905, at the prison. During that interview, he said, Leon had confessed that he had lied in his testimony at Mary's trial to save his own life. Another affidavit from Bennington undertaker James Walbridge claimed that he had found a compound fracture in the skull of Marcus Rogers, contradicting the belief that he had been killed by asphyxiation.

The evidence of the appeal affidavits quickly collapsed, decisively undermined by the counterarguments of prosecutor Orion Barber and Vermont attorney general Clark C. Fitts. They produced testimony impugning the professional reputation of Dr. MacWayne and noted that there was a plethora of evidence to prove that Mary had been in Bennington on August 10, 1902, not in MacWayne's Hoosick Falls office. Further investigation of Leon Perham's January 31 interview, moreover, revealed that while he *had* admitted lying at Mary's trial, he never specified exactly *what* he lied about. And undertaker Walbridge's assertion was dismissed as improbable; a compound skull fracture could not have been missed by the autopsy physicians and must have been inflicted during their dissection of Marcus's corpse.

On May 19, 1905, the Vermont Supreme Court justices heard Mary's appeal, and on May 30 it was denied by a vote of 5 to 2, Justices Haselton and Powers dissenting. Mary's lawyers immediately asked Governor Bell for another reprieve in order to give them time to file a petition asking for a writ of error from the United States Supreme Court. Bell granted another reprieve, and the legal fight continued.

On November 6, 1905, lawyers T. L. Jeffords and F. M. Butler pleaded Mary Rogers's appeal before the U.S. Supreme Court. The case was concerned solely with technical issues having to do with her sentence and its execution by the Vermont courts. On November 27 Supreme Court Justice William R. Day handed down the decision denying Mary's last hope for legal salvation.

Mary's attitude seemed to improve after this last hope was dashed. Although she broke down and wept when informed of the Supreme Court ruling, she pulled herself together as preparations commenced for her scheduled hanging on December 8. In the aftermath of her sentencing, Mary had angrily spurned religious consolation; when her mother offered to bring her a Roman Catholic priest, Mary sputtered, "You can take your priest and go to hell. I have no use for him." She now relented, welcoming both Father Cornelius C. Delaney and Windsor Prison chaplain W. H. Hayes to her death-row cell. There, she spent the last two weeks of her life in the constant company of prison official Merton Loukes and his wife, who mounted a vigilant suicide watch on their prisoner. Margaret, the Loukeses' four-year-old daughter, was also often in Mary's cell, and it was said that her childish prattle furnished blessed distraction to the preoccupied woman. Mary also whiled away her remaining time by crocheting aprons, her gifts to those who had sent her money and messages of support during her long imprisonment.

Crocheting was not all Mary was up to during her long prison sojourn. During the last half of 1905, the Windsor Prison management was engulfed by heavily publicized scandals. A panel appointed by Governor Bell found widespread peculation, corruption, and irregular procedures at the prison, and several prison officials were disgraced and fired. The most sensational revelations of the prison probe, however, concerned Mary Rogers. In late August it was disclosed that Vernon Rogers, a convicted rapist acting as a prison "trusty," had enjoyed access to Mary's cell and person during the first half of the previous March. Owing to the laxity of prison officials, Vernon Rogers had gained access to a key that fitted the front locks of Mary's cell. She, for her part, had procured a pair of sewing scissors, which she used to dismantle the locks on her side of the cell door. The result was unfettered fraternization for a period of ten days, during which, Mary admitted in a signed confession, she had sexual intercourse several times with Vernon Rogers.

The disclosure of her jail sex came at the worst possible time for Mary Rogers. Public gossip that she was in the family way had been repeatedly denied by prison officials, especially the rumor that they had deliberately allowed male prisoners sexual access to her in the hope that she would beat the hangman by becoming pregnant. The Vernon Rogers scandal seemed verification of such rumors and continuing evidence that Mary was an unrepentant loose woman, rather than the simple-minded damsel in distress painted by her supporters. At least one Mary Rogers scholar, Clinton Krauss, believes that the public reaction to the Vernon Rogers scandal was a critical element in the failure to save Mary Rogers from the gallows.

The question remains, however: Was Mary Rogers pregnant at the time of her death? Although the claim was made by her partisans, there is no clear evidence that she was with child when she stepped to the scaffold. She apparently *was* pregnant at the time she murdered her husband, which may have influenced her emotional condition and given additional urgency to her plan. She apparently lost that child through miscarriage while incarcerated.

During the first week of December, preparations for Mary's

hanging went smoothly forward. Her gallows, which had already been assembled and disassembled twice as successive reprieves came through, was once again removed from the prison attic and set up in the interior yard. It had last been used in 1891, and its parts were numbered so that it could be easily assembled in about thirty minutes. Constructed of solid oak, it rose to a height of eight feet from its platform, a ten-by-eight-foot rectangle. Its drop was about two feet square, and the fall through it was calculated at about six feet. The entire structure was painted black and coated with thick varnish. The rope was made of hemp and was three-quarters of an inch thick. Both the drop and rope were tested two days before the hanging to prevent any ugly mishap.

Five days before her death, Mary's mother and her half-sister Catherine visited her for the last time in her cell. Their journey to Windsor was apparently underwritten by the *Boston Messenger* newspaper, which paid their expenses in return for exclusive rights to their stories. This was a reflection of worldwide interest in the Rogers case, as the hanging of a woman, being highly unusual, was "good copy" for the Hearst-style newspapers of the era. Such "yellow press" methods did not sit well with staid Vermonters unused to the sensationalistic approach of the metropolitan dailies. When a newspaper photographer attempted to take pictures of the mother and sister as they left the prison, Superintendent Lovell forbade any photography and ordered the newspapermen off the prison grounds. The *St. Albans Messenger* correspondent, who may have wished to justify to his own editor his relative lack of access, was vituperative in his excoriation of his competitors:

> As an illustration of the measures to which the sensational yellow press will resort for the manufacture of degenerate reading material for the morbidly curious, the visit of the mother and

sister of Mrs. Rogers to the prison today is a fair sample. . . . the brutally revolting fact is that this simple old woman and her daughter are unconsciously made to play the part of mere play figures in a cruel little puppet show that is certainly outrageously sensational. Boston newspapers concocted in order that the occurrence might be written up and fed to the public as news. Briefly and bluntly, Mary Rogers' own mother apparently has been acting as the representative of a certain yellow newspaper, had the entrée of the death chamber and furnished no end of "stories" and yet probably does not even realize how she has been duped, nor how basely her private sorrow has been made mere public capital for lurid newspaper sensationalism.

The efforts to save Mary's life continued to the bitter end. Thanks in great part to the tireless campaigning of Mrs. William J. Blickensderfer of Connecticut, a self-appointed Rogers champion, Governor Bell was deluged with petitions from all over the United States demanding he commute Mary's death sentence. Typical of such heartfelt effusions was a letter from the board of the United Women of the Republic in Cleveland. Signed by Mrs. Stephen Buhrer, the wife of a former Cleveland mayor, the letter focused on the barbarity of capital punishment, especially for a woman, and concluded, "It would be a shame and a disgrace in this enlightened day to execute a woman who for her actions was irresponsible at all times." Percival W. Clement, the Vermont Republican Party machine candidate for governor, tried to make Mary's doom a campaign issue, demanding that Governor Bell stop her execution. Such efforts continued to the last minute, with Bell granting a hearing to Mary's appeal attorneys Charles A. McCarthy and E. B. Flinn at 8 AM on her death day. After hearing them out, Bell stated that the facts did not warrant any further delay. And it is only fair to say that, notwithstanding the frantic campaign to save Mary Rogers, Bell may well have represented majority opinion concerning Mary

Rogers. Buried in a dusty file at the Vermont Historical Society Center in Barre is a file of letters applauding Bell's decision to let the Rogers execution go forward. Typical of such effusions was the letter of Brattleboro attorney James Hooker, who, like most partisans on either side of the Rogers controversy, invoked the Deity to support his views, writing, "If ever a person deserved hanging this wretch did and I thank God the law has been vindicated." No less effusive was the praise of second-year Harvard law students Carroll M. Perkins and John B. Roberts, who stated they took "honest pride as citizens of New England" in Bell's steely implementation of the law.

Mary played her part well in the final grisly scenes. After a good night's sleep, she awoke at 5 AM and dressed herself without aid. She then labored over a last note to prison superintendent Lovell. It read:

Dear Mr. Lovell,—As I am not much in speaking, I pen you a few words as an expression of my extreme gratefulness for your extreme friendness [sic] bestowed upon me since in your care. Mr. Lovell, I may not always have done as well as I might have done, perhaps, but my only means of atonement now for what is past is to tell you that I am sorry and heartily sorry. I know that you have a very kind heart and I am bound to think that I may obtain from you forgiveness.

You know that Jesus tells us "If thy brother trespass against thee and turn again to thee saying I repent, forgive him. Be ye tender-hearted and forgiving, even as God for Christ's sake has forgiven you in his name." Mabel

Refuting the cliché about the condemned eating heartily, Mary skipped both breakfast and lunch on her last day on earth.

It appears that the other actors in Mary's final scene may not have played their parts as well as she. Although there were at least forty spectators to her death, descriptions of Mary's last moments differed widely. The real truth may never be known, as the only official account of her execution was a very nominal release written by a committee of three reporters, the only representatives of the press allowed into the prison by Superintendent Lovell. Other supposedly eyewitness descriptions, however, eventually leaked out, and they suggested that the affair was, at least to some extent, botched. Owing either to an unforeseen elasticity in the hemp rope or the miscalculated weight of Mary's body, the rope stretched so much as she fell through the drop that her feet were seen to hit the ground below. Prison officials denied that her feet remained there, claiming that she bounced back up in the air. Other witnesses, however, stated that it was found necessary for Deputies H. A. Bond and P. C. Tinkham to grab the rope above Mary and hold it up for the entire fourteen minutes it took her to die. This account was angrily denied by prison officials and also by one of Mary's original lawyers, Daniel Guiltinan, who witnessed her death. In any case, her execution clearly malfunctioned at the most basic level, as her neck was not broken by the initial drop, and the forty witnesses watched uncomfortably as she painfully strangled to death. One of the attending deputies was later quoted as saying, "I had to turn away my head. May I never be commanded to take part in another such undertaking."

Dr. Dean Richmond, the prison physician, stood by Mary's body as it writhed in its death convulsions. Eleven minutes after she dropped, he could hear no heartbeat, and he pronounced her dead at 1:27 PM. Her body was immediately placed in a coffin by undertaker Louis Haussler and hurried to the Windsor train station forty-five minutes later. There, before a curious crowd of spectators, it was put on a train to Hoosick Falls. Several hours later it arrived there but was taken off before the train arrived at the station, to avoid a crowd of the morbidly curious gathered there. The next morning, with only her mother, her three sisters, and a dozen other spectators present, Mary's body was interred without funeral rites in St. Mary's Cemetery.

The execution of Mary Rogers did not put an end to arguments about her degree of guilt. Although it was not brought up at her original trial, the burden of Mary's subsequent defense was that she was either insane or at least not intelligent enough to be legally responsible for killing Marcus Rogers. As Mary came closer and closer to the gallows, more and more persons came forward to insist that her whole family was notorious for mental instability and that she herself had never been better than a "half-wit." (Judging from the trial record, the same could have been said of Marcus Rogers, Stella Bates, Morris Knapp, and both Perham brothers.) Suffice it to say that Mary Rogers was probably mentally deficient, virtually uneducated, and not intelligent enough to cover the least of her tracks in the clumsy plotting of her husband's death. The last word on the Rogers case therefore should go to the anonymous *Bennington Banner* reporter who covered her trial and sentencing for the hometown crowd. Commenting on Mary's seemingly cold, calculated courtroom demeanor, the journalist acknowledged popular perceptions of her "unwomanly" persona, but offered this persuasive demurral: "The impression she gave the reporter was that she is a stupid, ignorant woman, whose stupidity has been mistaken for nerve."

CHAPTER 4

"A MIXED CASE OF PICKLES"

The 1929 Chester Mystery

Vermonters of 1929 called it the Chester Mystery, and it was, as one discerning reporter remarked, quite a "mixed case of pickles." At first it looked like murder, then suicide. Then officials couldn't identify the corpse—but as soon as they put a name to it, that person turned up embarrassingly alive. George J. Packard, the man at the middle of the mystery, appeared to be a widower—only to be revealed as a man with two wives. More puzzling yet, we *still* don't know what poor woman lies under an anonymous gravestone in the potter's field of Chester Township's Pleasant View Cemetery —except that it definitely wasn't Catherine Rockwell Packard.

It all began in farmer Robert Field's pasture, just a couple miles outside Chester village in Windsor County. It was the afternoon of August 20, 1929, and Field was taking his usual shortcut through a small spruce grove to retrieve his cows, when he almost stumbled over the rotting body of a young woman. He quickly summoned Windsor County sheriff Ernest Schoenfeld and town health officer Dr. John A. Stevenson. Despite their best efforts, however, the men could make little sense of the grisly scene.

The badly decomposed corpse had obviously been lying there, facedown, for some time. It was the body of a young woman, apparently in her mid-twenties. About five feet, four inches in height, and weighing about 110 pounds, she had brown hair and a long, thin face with a heavy lower jaw. The most distinguishing feature of the corpse was its dental condition. An upper eyetooth and incisor were gold-capped, and the mouth was missing a total of twelve teeth.

The other details and circumstances of the corpse furnished no additional clues to her identity. When found, she was dressed in a fur-collared three-quarter-length tan coat of a tweedy basket weave, a sweaterlike jacket, a dress of reddish pink silk with a black braid hem, silk underwear, rolled stockings, and black high-heeled shoes. Pinned to her dress was a cheap piece of costume jewelry, a brooch in the shape of a horseshoe. There were no identifying tags on any of her garments.

It didn't take long for investigating officials to reach a consensus on the cause of death. A partially empty chloroform bottle was found by the side of the woman, and a green hat and a stocking, apparently once saturated with chloroform, were discovered still adhering to her skull. Also found by the corpse was a leather purse. In it were 38 cents, an unopened bottle of iodine, and a note dated June 19, 1929. It read: "I am sick of life and I am going where I will be happy."

After performing an autopsy on August 21, Dr. Fred S. Kent of the State Laboratory of Hygiene ruled the death a suicide. Most Chester Township and Windsor County officials agreed with him, although Chester physician Dr. George X. Roberts dissented, insisting that it was more likely a case of murder. He argued strongly, if in vain, that the one ounce missing from the three-ounce chloroform bottle was an amount insufficient to have caused death.

Kent's verdict helped little in solving the puzzle of the dead woman's identity. Responding to statewide publicity about the case, Chester residents Oscar and Bertha Johnson came forward to say that they had seen a young female resembling the dead woman's photograph walking near Robert Field's pasture on June 19, the presumed death date. They had offered her a ride but she had simply replied, "No thanks, I have not far to go," and continued walking. The Johnsons also recalled later seeing an empty automobile with New Hampshire license plates near the scene. But no one came forward to identify or claim the corpse, and publicized appeals to Vermont's dentists to identify its dental work were fruitless. After holding the body for six days, Chester officials buried it in the potter's field at Pleasant View Cemetery and filed away photographs of the corpse and the items found with it.

Ten months passed quietly by. In late June of 1930, a young man named George Joseph Packard stopped by the Chester Town Hall. Packard, a twenty-one-year-old Rutland candy store clerk, had recently heard about the Chester mystery, and he told Sheriff Schoenfeld that he suspected the Chester corpse was none other than his twenty-one-year-old wife, Catherine Rockwell Packard, who had disappeared from their Rutland home in April 1929. After examining the photographs and the clothing and brooch found on the corpse, George Packard positively identified the dead woman as his wife, and the suicide note as being in her handwriting. Her death, he opined to Vermont state detective Edwin C. Brown before leaving Chester, must have been a murder, as she had held a strong religious aversion to suicide.

It soon developed that George Packard wasn't the only party interested in positively identifying Catherine Packard. Mary Agnes Packard, George's mother, held a $459 insurance policy on the presumably deceased Catherine, and she now filed for payment with the John Hancock Mutual Life Insurance Company of Massachusetts.

Politely but firmly, the company refused to pay the claim, stating simply to Mary Packard and Chester town officials that they had a "reasonable belief that the body was not that of Mrs. Packard."

Undeterred by such flinty-hearted skepticism, George Packard moved decisively to get on with his life. His two young children, now living with his parents, needed a mother, and he had not been mourning Catherine to any great excess. Less than three weeks after identifying his wife's corpse, George Packard married Margaret L. MacFarland in a midnight ceremony in Rutland.

Alas for George and Margaret, their conjugal felicity did not last long. The redoubtable Mabel Abbott was another party interested in the whereabouts of Catherine Packard, and she had begun her own queries after seeing newspaper accounts of George's identification of the Chester corpse. Miss Abbott was no stranger to Catherine, having spent some years guiding her development and destiny after the orphaned Catherine became a ward of the Vermont Children's Aid Society at the age of thirteen. Knowing Catherine as she did, Abbott didn't believe for a moment that she lay under a potter's field stone in Chester, and as July 1930 waned into August, Abbott assiduously worked the network of their mutual acquaintances.

Abbott hit pay dirt in early August. Discovering that Catherine was currently in contact with persons in Manchester, New Hampshire, Abbott journeyed there. She quickly learned that Catherine was working as a family domestic and confronted her. Readily admitting her identity, Catherine expressed astonishment that she had ever been presumed dead and agreed to return with Abbott to Vermont to clear up matters.

The news of Catherine Packard's resurrection burst upon a surprised world on Thursday, August 14, 1930, when she returned in Miss Abbott's custody to Bellows Falls and thence to Springfield, where she was jailed, in lieu of $2,000 bail, as a material witness in the investigation of the Chester corpse. Making headlines throughout the United States, Catherine's reappearance was widely sensationalized as a true-life, modern-day "Enoch Arden" tale (a reference to the Tennyson poem of the same name, which relates the melancholy tale of a presumably dead husband who returns to find his wife remarried). Among the shocked, naturally, were newlyweds George and Margaret Packard, who announced, respectively, "I can't believe it," and "I am astonished," before speeding with George's children to Springfield to meet with Catherine. More prudently, George also secured the services of an attorney for the coming struggle.

That domestic confrontation, nicely orchestrated by Vermont attorney general J. Ward Carver and Windsor County state's attorney Lawrence C. Edgerton, occurred on Friday, August 15, and handsomely fulfilled the hopes of the journalists who chronicled it. Espying her children, George Jr., now age three, and Helen Mary, one and a half, Catherine burst into edifying tears when she realized that Helen—who had been but a few months old when her mother abandoned her—did not recognize her. But Catherine soon calmed down and the adults quickly sorted out the main elements in their complicated family conundrum. They subsequently announced to reporters a sensibly amicable settlement of the major issues: George would divorce Catherine, while Margaret would seek an annulment of her now-invalid marriage to George so that they could be remarried legally. It all seemed to have been an unfortunate misunderstanding and those involved would now smoothly resume the even tenor of their former lives.

Such a smooth resolution must have seemed too good to be true —and it was. The projected bundle of happy endings began to disintegrate as details of Catherine's former life and her post-disappearance wanderings leaked out to an avid press and public.

Many of the most damning details were furnished, not surprisingly, by her disenchanted mother-in-law, Mary Agnes Packard. Catherine's initial explanation of her whereabouts, it developed, was a tissue of lies and half-truths. She had not disappeared from her Rutland home because she needed to find work "out west"; she had simply abandoned her husband and children without warning on April 13, 1929, and left for Cleveland, Ohio. Not once had she subsequently gotten in touch with her children or inquired as to their welfare. Soon after departing Vermont, she had teamed up— possibly by prearrangement—with a former acquaintance named Robert ("Romeo") King, also an alleged friend of her husband's and one who supposedly helped George "search" for his missing spouse.

Things had gone from bad to worse during Catherine and Robert's ensuing year on the road. They lived first in Cleveland before moving on to Erie, Pennsylvania. After Robert lost his job at the General Electric plant there, they motored eastward in his truck. Depending on whose version you believed, that truck either broke down for good in rural Pennsylvania or was repossessed for nonpayment of its installment loans. Whatever its fate, its loss triggered Catherine and Robert's final falling-out. Deaf to his pleas that she remain and possibly even a veiled threat ("You might get what the rest of them got"), Catherine hitchhiked to Manchester, where she secured employment as a maid. Following Catherine's further interrogation by lawmen, several of the itinerant playmates of her missing year were rounded up by police. Besides Robert King, who turned himself in to police at Concord, New Hampshire, they included Hilda Walbridge and Harrison Smith. All were jailed as material witnesses in the reopened probe of the Chester mystery death.

As far as Vermont authorities were concerned, the most tantalizing link between Catherine Packard and the Chester dead woman was the suicide note found with the corpse. Perhaps it was true, as Catherine doggedly insisted, that she had no knowledge of the dead woman. And perhaps it was likewise true that George Packard had identified the corpse in the sincere belief that it was his dead wife— a conviction possibly enhanced by his anxiety to wed Margaret MacFarland. But what couldn't be easily explained was how a suicide note apparently written by Catherine Packard had ended up in a purse next to the dead body in Robert Field's pasture. George's belief at the time that the note was definitely in his wife's handwriting was echoed by Boston handwriting expert William E. Hingston. And Catherine herself now admitted that she had written not just one, but several suicide notes similar to the one found with the Chester victim. She told her interrogators that she had often suffered bouts of despondency after her 1926 marriage to George Packard, and that it was possible the dead woman had somehow come into possession of one such note and used it for her own fatal purpose.

The Chester case just got curiouser and curiouser as the next week sped by. Once it was clear that the dead woman was not Catherine Packard, a dozen other candidates were proposed, with varying degrees of fervency. Their names were furnished from all over New England, where many a grieving mother dreaded the possibility that the Chester victim might be their own missing or estranged daughter. One such mother was Susan Strain of Cornish, New Hampshire, who was ultimately pleased to find her daughter very much alive—but mortified to discover she was one of Catherine's disreputable friends, the jailed Hilda Walbridge. Another distraught parent was the mother of Anna Little, who now came forward to say that her long-missing daughter had once been an intimate of Robert King. Two other potential claimants were Sophie Courtney of Manchester, seeking her daughter Elizabeth, and Mrs. A. J.

Bogart of Troy, New York, searching for her long-lost daughter Esther. Still farther afield, another possible candidate for the deceased was Matilda Anderson of Boston, who had been missing for more than a year.

On August 19, state's attorney Edgerton announced the most promising clue yet in the frustrating Chester puzzle. Making public a letter from Mrs. Belle Chickering of Hardwick, he echoed her contention that the Chester corpse was probably that of her daughter, Ruby Chickering Green. Missing since November of 1926, Ruby had worked in various places as a nurse and had last been heard from in Utica, New York. More interestingly, she was no stranger to the Chester area and had once worked on a farm there. In addition, Ruby's dental records were a pretty good match for those of the Chester corpse. While working in Chester in 1921, Ruby had contracted both typhoid fever and tetanus. She had been rushed to the Mary Fletcher Hospital in Burlington and had ten of her teeth extracted during the course of her treatment there. It wasn't much of a stretch to assume that she could easily have lost two more teeth before arriving in Chester on her final, fatal errand of June 19, 1929. Better yet, she was about five feet, four inches in height, and known samples of Ruby's handwriting were very similar to both that of Catherine Packard and the writing in the suicide note. And although there was no record of her working at the same Troy, New York, orphanage where Catherine Packard was employed in 1929, Catherine eventually told police she thought she remembered a woman resembling Ruby Green there at the time. Not only that, but Catherine also helpfully recalled that the woman had a purse the same color as that found with the Chester corpse!

Ruby Chickering Green had endured a sad life. Leland Green, the father of her three children, had been sent to prison after a conviction on a morals charge in 1920. Two of her children became wards of the state, and Ruby subsequently drifted from one temporary job to another through the first half of the 1920s. So Belle Chickering's scenario seemed a highly plausible one: Ruby Green, depressed by her husband's betrayal, the loss of her children, and ill health, had returned to Chester, a place where she had once been relatively happy, and killed herself in Robert Field's pasture.

Fictional mysteries are invariably well-plotted and decisively resolved. Real-life mysteries often remain unsolved and ambiguous. The Chester Mystery, alas, is one such puzzle. If the Chester suicide was Ruby Chickering Green, we will never know for sure. Despite a reward of $200 offered by Vermont governor John E. Weeks for the positive identification of the Chester corpse, no one ever collected that sum. And although state's attorney Edgerton pronounced himself "satisfied" that the Chester victim was Ruby Green, no one ever went to the trouble of exhuming the Chester corpse, although many would-be detectives responded ephemerally to police pleas for aid in resolving the case. One such volunteer sleuth, a woodchopper of Windsor County, touted his credentials to lawmen thusly: "I have always wanted to be [a] secret service man and trail down such mysteries as this Chester case. I have studied the work and trailed down other cases." Ultimately, however, no one came forward to offer proof of the corpse's identity, and it remains unknown to this day.

Meanwhile, the rosy future plotted by the case's principals continued to deteriorate. As promised, George J. Packard quickly filed for a divorce from Catherine, a decree for which was granted on September 26, 1930, on grounds of adultery. Less than a month later, George and Margaret MacFarland were reunited in holy wedlock in a Burlington ceremony. Catherine's immediate fate, however, was not so blessed. Following her prolonged grilling by Vermont lawmen and the arrest of yet another of her sexual playmates, Fred

Bunker of Springfield, both Bunker and Catherine were arraigned before Judge Glen Howland in the Windsor Municipal Court on August 29, 1930. Despite representation by court-appointed attorney Louis G. Whitcomb, the two were briskly convicted on charges of adultery. Margaret was sentenced to six months to three years in the Rutland Reformatory for Women, while Fred earned a one-to-three-year term in Windsor Prison. The charges against the remaining defendants were eventually dropped, and the public turned its attention to such matters as the continuing economic downturn.

This is where the story ends, except for a couple of odd post-scripts. None of George J. Packard's marriages, it would seem, were made in heaven. His third marriage, perhaps not astonishingly, lasted longer than his first two put together. It, too, however, ended on September 1, 1953, the decree being granted on the then-customary ground of "intolerable severity." A far more bizarre fate was the destiny of Catherine Rockwell Packard. Several years after paying her debt to society, she, too, took a second chance in the lottery of marriage. Perhaps justly suspicious of strangers, she married a little closer to home than her erstwhile spouse. Catherine's second husband, believe it or not, was sixty-four-year-old Horace Packard, her ex-father-in-law and the sire of her first husband. They were united a little over eighteen months after Horace's wife, Catherine Agnes, succumbed to nephritis and heart disease. Perhaps it was a happy ending for the unfortunate Catherine, perhaps not. All we can be sure of is that her destiny was better than that of the anonymous woman who still sleeps in a pauper's grave in Chester.

CHAPTER 5

DON'T KILL OVER SPILT MILK

The 1957 Orville Gibson Tragedy

They came for Orville Gibson in his barn shortly after 4 AM. It was December 31, 1957, and his killers knew that Gibson, like any other Vermont dairy farmer, would be there, tending his herd of a hundred dairy cows. There was probably a struggle: The mute evidence of a battered milk tin and a suggestive trail of silage hinted that Gibson fought his captors before he was overwhelmed. Perhaps it was there they trussed him, tying his feet together and binding his hands behind his knees. They then dragged him out three hundred feet to U.S. Route 5 and hustled him into a waiting automobile, most likely into the trunk. His abductors drove north for a half-mile before turning right, toward the bridge that connects Newbury, Vermont, to Haverhill, New Hampshire. Gibson was probably unconscious when they took him out of the trunk. One hopes so—for they then hoisted him up on the south parapet of the bridge and dumped him into the cold, swirling waters of the Connecticut River. A minute later there was no sign of either Orville Gibson or his murderers.

The Orville Gibson murder was the most shocking Vermont

murder of the 1950s. And Vermonters weren't the only Americans horrified by its brutal details. The Gibson homicide and its ensuing trials garnered nationwide newspaper headlines for two years and provoked much soul-searching as to just what kind of place Vermont really was. It wasn't just the shock of the murder: a respectable citizen kidnapped out of his own barn, bound like an animal, and hurled helpless into the water to drown. Americans had grown used to such outrages, particularly as the civil rights movement arose in the South and atrocities like the Emmett Till lynching began to shock the national conscience. What made the Gibson murder so appalling to many citizens was its locale and context. It was bad enough that it happened in Newbury, Vermont, a seemingly perfect paradigm of a bucolic and neighborly New England farming town. But what truly shocked Vermonters and flatlanders alike was the inescapable inference that the Gibson murder had been, as one investigator termed it, a "community affair": a murder sanctioned and concealed by many residents of the victim's hometown.

Evalyn Gibson, Orville's wife, became worried when he didn't show up as usual for breakfast at 5 AM. Looking for him in the barn, she found the crushed milk pail but no sign of her husband. By 7:30 AM she had contacted the Vermont State Police and the hunt for Orville Gibson was on. Directed by Orange County state's attorney Harvey ("Bud") B. Otterman Jr. and aided by Lieutenant Chester Nash of the Vermont State Police and Orange County sheriff Russell Bagley, it quickly mushroomed into one of the greatest manhunts in Vermont history.

Investigators had little to work with. Indeed, with no witnesses to Gibson's disappearance or inklings of his whereabouts, they weren't sure initially whether it was foul play or a missing-person case. Had Gibson voluntarily vanished, for unknown personal reasons? It seemed unlikely: By all accounts he was a prosperous farmer without oppressive debts who kept pretty much to himself and had no scandalous entanglements or personal enemies. Well, almost none. Practically everyone in the western half of Orange County had been talking for a week about the Eri Martin affair. Martin, a fifty-seven-year-old hired hand, lived with his family in a house on the Gibson property. On Christmas Day afternoon there had been an altercation between Gibson and Martin in the barn. The participants' accounts of the affair differed radically, but there was no disputing the outcome, which left Martin with three broken ribs, an injured kidney, and multiple bruises. Indeed, Gibson was set to appear in Orange County Court on January 7 to face an assault charge brought by Martin. But no one who knew Gibson believed that his court problem was enough to motivate him to vanish. Yet, at the same time, there were no indisputable signs of violence in the barn. What in the world had happened to Orville Gibson?

Otterman and his sleuths worked hard to unravel the puzzle. Employing numerous Vermont state troopers, New Hampshire lawmen, Orange County sheriff's deputies, and civilian volunteers, they methodically searched the surrounding region during the following week. All 106 miles of Newbury town roads were combed, with special scrutiny of culverts, abandoned houses, and outbuildings. Searchers in boats fruitlessly dragged miles of the Connecticut River for Gibson's corpse, and every bus terminal, trucking depot, and train station was searched. Meanwhile, back at the Gibson farm, a bloodhound named Major failed to find Gibson's trail, as did state troopers who stopped and interrogated every motorist passing by the farm during a nine-hour period. No one, it seemed, knew what had happened to the missing Newbury farmer.

Otterman and his sleuths pressed on, increasingly mindful of criticism, especially by observers outside the Newbury area, that the sluggish pace of their investigation was hampered by community-wide resistance to the probe. Hundreds of persons were questioned by lawmen, most of the interrogations being conducted by two-man teams in rooms rented for the purpose at a Bradford motel. Additionally, at least sixty-two lie detector tests were administered to persons of interest in the case, including Gibson's wife and other relatives. Otterman insisted that local residents were cooperating fully with his investigators—but weeks, then months, went by with no break in the case. As March gave way to April, the only elements clearly understood were that Orville Gibson remained missing and that the probable motive for his disappearance was community anger over the Martin incident. In her comments after his disappearance, Evalyn Gibson had painted a pacific portrait of her husband. But that wasn't the Orville Gibson that Otterman's investigators heard tell of during their endless interviews. Whatever the truth about the Christmas Day fight with Eri Martin, it was clear that local residents were incensed to the point of fury over the incident. During the week before Gibson's disappearance, one local resident had even publicly recommended a dose of "tar and feathers" for Gibson, and it was clear that he had been widely perceived as something of a "bully of the town" even before his dustup with Martin.

The first break in the case came eighty-five days after Gibson vanished. The freezing over of the Connecticut River in early January had forced police to suspend dragging for a corpse, but Troopers Lawrence Washburn and William Graham decided on March 26 it was safe to resume the operation. It was a wise hunch. Joined by Bradford resident Patrick Quinn, the troopers reopened the search that morning, and at 11:20 AM the three men spotted Gibson's body from a boat near the New Hampshire shore, about a half-mile north of the bridge between Bradford, Vermont, and Piermont, New Hampshire. At 4:30 that afternoon a macabre procession hauled Gibson's body over the snow on an improvised sled to a waiting ambulance, which sped it to the A. E. Hale funeral parlor in Bradford. There Vermont state pathologist Richard S. Woodruff labored well into the next morning on a painstaking and thoroughly documented autopsy.

The results of Gibson's autopsy immediately turned Otterman's investigation into a murder probe. Ruling that the condition of the body indicated Gibson had died of asphyxiation, "cause unknown," Woodruff noted that there was no water in the lungs and only an insignificant exterior wound, a small cut on the right cheek. Moreover, the ropes that had hog-tied Gibson were still tight after almost three months in the water, all but ruling out the possibility of suicide. Woodruff surmised Gibson had been fatally choked with a scarf or pillow, as strangulation by human hands would probably have broken some bones.

Three days later Orville Gibson was laid to rest in the Oxbow Cemetery along Route 5. Meanwhile, Otterman's reenergized investigation went forward. By now virtually all lawmen agreed that the likely motive for Gibson's abduction and murder was community anger over the Martin beating. Otterman himself described it to reporters as "more or less a community affair," in which three to five men from the area had been involved. But despite Otterman's insistence that virtually all local citizens were cooperating with his investigation, the Gibson murder probe again stalled. More persons were interrogated, more submitted to lie detector tests, and greater efforts were made to find additional physical evidence. But the summer of 1958 turned to fall, and fall began to wane toward winter with seemingly nothing new in the case.

As suddenly as the shock of Gibson's disappearance came the news on November 5, 1958, that two suspects had been arrested. A fortnight later, Newbury elementary school janitor Robert Ozro

Welch, age forty-five, and Frank Whitman Carpenter, forty-two, a West Newbury mill hand, were arraigned for the Gibson murder. Charged with counts of kidnapping, manslaughter, and first-degree murder, the two men posted $40,000 bail each and secured the services of first-rate attorneys, Peter P. Plante of White River Junction representing Welch and Richard E. Davis of Barre acting for Carpenter. Several months later, Governor Robert T. Stafford announced that the case would be prosecuted by Vermont attorney general Frederick M. Reed, assisted by Harvey Otterman and state's attorney John Morale of Wells River. It was also determined that Welch and Carpenter would be tried separately.

Some trials are decided well before they begin. Both the prosecution and defense in the Robert Welch case tried hard, with preemptive maneuverings, to ensure a favorable outcome. On February 17, 1959, Judge Rudolf J. Daley of the Orange County Court approved a defense motion to allow Welch's lawyers to take depositions from the state's witnesses. Attorney General Reed parried with an appeal to the Vermont Supreme Court, which granted a temporary stay of the defense motion. The court's final ruling came on June 18, when Chief Justice Benjamin L. Hulburd denied the defense motion, stating that such a procedure "would in practical effect abrogate laws which provide for the controlled secrecy of grand jury and inquest proceedings."

Defense attorneys Plante and Henry Black, Plante's assisting counsel for the Welch trial, had just begun to fight. Two weeks before the opening of Welch's trial on October 6, Plante filed additional motions, requesting defense access to all physical evidence in the case, a copy of the autopsy report, the results of Welch's polygraph examination, all photographs in the state's possession, and a list of the prosecution witnesses. He also renewed a request for transcripts of the grand jury's probe. Attorney General Reed countered on September 30 with a motion to consolidate the kidnapping and murder charges against Welch into one count. Reed's justification for his motion was that it would save "time, expense and agitation" in what already promised to be a prolonged trial. Presiding Judge Natt L. Divoll Jr. made short work of them all, denying the prosecution request to consolidate the counts against Welch and denying defense motions for access to grand jury proceedings and a last-minute plea for a continuance of the trial. But Divoll did grant the defense requests for the autopsy report, photographs, and the lie detector results.

Finally, almost two years after Gibson's murder, the Welch trial got under way at 9:30 AM on Tuesday, October 6, 1959, at the Orange County Courthouse in Chelsea. Jury selection is probably the most tedious aspect of criminal trials, and the Welch trial was no exception. Beginning that Tuesday, and continuing over the following three days, more than one hundred persons were examined. As expected, most of the questions directed at them by Attorney General Reed and Harvey Otterman pertained to their views on capital punishment and the weight of circumstantial evidence in capital cases. (In 1959 Vermont juries sitting in first-degree murder cases could choose between execution and life imprisonment in capital cases.). Finally, on Friday, October 9, the selection process was complete, and Judge Divoll charged the jury.

Prosecutor Reed promptly opened with a strong statement of the state's case against Robert O. Welch. While admitting that the evidence was largely circumstantial, Reed asserted that the killing of Gibson stemmed from community outrage over the beating of Eri Martin. Reed noted that three days after the fight, Robert Welch, like many another Newbury citizen, had visited Martin and offered sympathy. But unlike many another Newbury citizen, Reed continued, Welch had *never* visited Martin before. Nor had he ever said, according to Martin, what he said to the bedridden Martin on December 28, which were the heartfelt words, "Someone ought to give Gibson a dose of his own medicine." Having established a plausible motive, Reed stated that the murder of Gibson had occurred during the commission of a felony, a clear implication that the attack on Gibson may not have been intentionally lethal but had somehow turned deadly as Gibson battled his attackers. Reed concluded by promising to prove that the rope used to hog-tie Gibson belonged to Robert Welch and that the state had an eyewitness who saw him near Gibson's home at the time of the murder.

In response to Reed's opening, Henry Black replied that the defense would reserve its statement, particularly as its evidence and arguments would differ radically from those of the state. The court then recessed, the tightly sequestered jury filing out for dinner in the basement of the Congregational Church before retiring to their rooms at the Colonial Inn.

When court resumed on Monday, October 12, the state's first witness, Eri Martin, testified. Martin had never been a suspect in the case, being bedridden at the time of Gibson's disappearance. But Attorney General Reed trusted that his account of his beating would support the state's contention that the incident had sparked community vengeance against Gibson, with Welch as its chief agent. Reed led Martin carefully through the events of Christmas Day afternoon. Martin admitted that he had been drinking at the time, and his condition led to his spilling two eighty-five-pound containers of milk. Some time later he had asked Gibson what he was going to do about the spilt milk, and Gibson insisted Martin would have to pay for it. The enraged Martin began shouting, then took off his hat and stamped on it. Gibson, in turn, lost his temper, struck Martin in the face, and then shoved him out of the barn, using his knee for encouragement. But Martin's testimony was mitigated during cross-examination when Black got him to admit that Gibson had never previously threatened or struck him during his five-year tenure at the farm. Before stepping down, however, Martin corroborated the state's contention that Welch had visited him after the incident and suggested that Gibson deserved a "dose of his own medicine."

The state next put former state legislator Walter B. Renfrew on the stand. Despite rancorous quibbling over whom he had said it to, Renfrew readily admitted that he had recommended a little "tar and feathering" for Gibson in his conversations with aroused area residents in the week after Martin's beating. As the state had hoped, his testimony helped establish the vindictive currents swirling around Orville Gibson in his final days. Renfrew was followed by Evalyn Gibson, Gibson's brother-in-law Freeman Placey, and State Troopers Washburn and Graham, all of whom filled in the meager details of Gibson's disappearance and the discovery of his body. Black peppered Reed's examination of virtually all his witnesses with emphatic objections, most of which were entered into the court record for possible appeal. Indeed, *Burlington Free Press* reporter Joe Heaney exaggerated little when he wrote that "Black objected to 95 per cent of the state proceedings."

Tuesday's court session got off to a slow start as state police corporal Ronald Woodward testified about photographs taken of Gibson's corpse at the time of its discovery. Next came dentist Leonard J. Abbadessa, who had identified Gibson's corpse by means of his dental records. Courtroom interest now perked up as state pathologist Richard S. Woodruff took the stand. After furnishing the gruesome details of his autopsy, he altered his original ruling and now stated Gibson had been alive when thrown into the Connecticut River and that his asphyxiation had been caused by drowning.

Late Tuesday afternoon, key witness state police lieutenant

Chester Nash began testifying. Despite Black's skillful badgering of him over alleged mistreatment of Welch during his March 28, 1958, interrogation, Nash eventually recounted confronting Welch with the rope used to hog-tie Orville Gibson and asking the janitor, "Is this your rope?" Nash didn't get a chance to continue, as Black violently objected and the jury was removed from the room. But after consulting with both sides, Judge Divoll ruled Nash's testimony admissible, and the next morning, he told the jury Welch's reaction when he saw the rope: "My God, fellows, that's my rope!"

Nash's dramatic revelation was the high point of the state's case. That case, however, began to unravel rapidly that Wednesday afternoon when Dr. John H. Perry-Hooker took the stand. Perry-Hooker testified that he had driven past the Gibson farm at about 3:15 AM on December 31. Shortly before passing it he had noticed a two-tone Kaiser automobile, which he thought he recognized as Frank Carpenter's. More important, as he passed the car he saw at least three persons in it, one of whom he recognized as Robert Welch and another as Frank Carpenter. But Perry-Hooker's testimony collapsed under Black's intense cross-examination. The dogged defense attorney first got him to renege on his positive identification of Carpenter, forcing a concession that he was "not entirely sure" about seeing Carpenter. More dramatically, in his last question to the beleaguered physician, Black got him to admit that he was nearsighted. Reed immediately elicited the acknowledgment that Perry-Hooker wore glasses, but the damage was done.

Court was delayed on Thursday morning, October 15, as defense counsels Black and Plante requested that the court instruct the jury to bring a directed verdict of acquittal. After conferring with the assisting trial judges, Henry Tillson and Kenneth Butler, Judge Divoll rejected Black's motion and asked the defense to open its case. Black countered by immediately resting the case and repeating his motion for a directed acquittal. Following another judicial conference, Divoll did precisely that, explaining to the jury that the state had simply not proved Welch's involvement in Gibson's disappearance or murder. Minutes later the jury returned with the acquittal, and suddenly it was all over, as Welch family members smothered each other and the defense attorneys with hugs. Not that it mattered much by then to Robert O. Welch. Noticeably pale during the trial, he entered the hospital for tests eleven days later. They indicated that he had leukemia, which killed him on December 20, 1958.

The apparent defeat suffered by state prosecutors only emboldened them to further exertions in their frustrating investigation. The renewed effort was partly spurred by the adverse comment generated nationwide by the Welch verdict. But no newspaper articulated the burden of such comment better than the one closest to the scene. As the *Bradford United Opinion* put it in an editorial after Welch's acquittal:

> Vermont and particularly this area of it have awakened this week in the harsh light that reveals the unsolved Gibson murder as "lynch law." From both within and outside the state in the last week has come strong editorial comment to the effect that there is no essential difference between a Vermont lynching or one in Mississippi—and that the murder "will remain a blot on Vermont's name and a cancer on Newbury's conscience until justice is served." That is strong talk—but deserved.

On November 5, 1959, Attorney General Reed opened a second, extremely secret grand-jury probe of the Gibson murder. Fresh witnesses were called, and more lie detector tests were administered. For all of that, however, the only significant issue of Reed's probe was a perjury indictment against one local resident. It soon became apparent that the last hope of justice might be the upcoming trial of Frank W. Carpenter. Reed, following his defeat at the Welch trial, had dropped the first-degree murder charge against Carpenter. But Carpenter still faced kidnapping and manslaughter charges.

Carpenter's long-delayed trial finally got under way on Monday morning, April 18, 1960. The presiding judge was F. Ray Keyser, assisted by Judges Tillson and Butler. Prosecuting for the state were Attorney General Thomas M. Debevoise and Orange County state's attorney John Morale; the defense attorneys were Richard E. Davis and Stephen Martin. Jury selection was a comparatively smooth process, both sets of attorneys mainly concerned with the prospective jurors' views on circumstantial evidence and whether they had read a sensationalistic treatment of the Gibson murder in *Cavalier Magazine*. The jury was filled by late Tuesday afternoon, a panel of seven women and five men. On Wednesday morning they were taken to view the crime scenes before testimony began that afternoon.

At the Carpenter trial there were many familiar faces and much the same testimony as at the Welch trial. Evalyn Gibson, Dr. Perry-Hooker, Eri Martin, and a host of state troopers repeated the stories they had told the previous October. But what was new at the Carpenter trial was the emphasis of both the prosecution and defense on scientific evidence. The state's forensic direction became clear when Dr. Richard Woodruff took the stand. His testimony was largely aimed at proving that the injuries to Gibson's body were inflicted before death—that is, in the commission of the felony kidnapping that led to it. Woodruff spent much of his eleven hours on the stand attempting to prove that the levels of carbon monoxide in Gibson's blood indicated he had possibly been exposed to it in an automobile trunk—most likely from the admittedly faulty muffler in Frank Carpenter's Kaiser. But Richard Davis brilliantly trumped Woodruff's testimony with the appearances of two expert witnesses of his own. The first was Dr. Joseph W. Spelman, a former Vermont state pathologist. Spelman had developed the very carbon monoxide tests used by Woodruff, and he now confessed to the jury, "I am ashamed to admit it, but my formula is both inadequate and inaccurate." The second was Dr. Richard Ford, acting director of the Harvard School of Legal Medicine. Ford successfully muddied Woodruff's testimony by telling the jury that the advanced state of decomposition in Gibson's body might have generated false carbon monoxide readings.

The state fared no better with its other expert witness, Dr. Harold C. Harrison, assistant director of criminal laboratories at the University of Rhode Island, who talked about microscopic fibers and paint chips found in the trunk of Carpenter's Kaiser. Projecting enlarged slides of the materials, Harrison indicated how they almost perfectly matched minute fibers and chips found on Gibson's clothing. Summarizing his comparisons, Harrison stated that Gibson's body was "probably" in the trunk of Carpenter's automobile. Davis riposted by putting William A. Johnson, a research physicist from the New England Laboratories in Ipswich, Massachusetts, on the stand. Like Spelman, he arraigned the inadequacy of the tests used by his counterpart, and suggested that the similarity of the paint particles might merely indicate that Gibson and Carpenter got their paint from the same source.

Worse yet for the state were the theatrics displayed by Dr. Richard Ford during his sensational appearance. Several witnesses had already raised the seemingly preposterous notion that Gibson had not been murdered, but had committed suicide. Ford took that notion over the top on Monday, May 2. Tying himself up exactly as Gibson had been trussed in just forty-five seconds, Ford told the jury that the condition of Ford's body was not inconsistent with suicide and that Gibson "most certainly" could have killed himself. The most important witnesses after Ford were several of Carpenter's relatives, all of whom swore he had been sleeping at home on the morning of December 31, 1957.

The trial was probably over the moment the trussed Ford tumbled to the courthouse floor, but it staggered through its motions to its end on Thursday night, May 5. After a little over three hours of deliberation, the jury found Carpenter innocent of the charges against him, and he was discharged by Judge Keyser.

More inconclusive legal rumblings, more caustic editorials, and even a story in *Life* magazine ensued after the Carpenter verdict. Ten years later, author Gerald Jay Goldberg published a fictionalized account of the affair, *The Lynching of Orin Newfield*. But the Gibson case basically ended with Carpenter's acquittal, almost two and a half years after the murder occurred. And properly so, at least as far as the two defendants were concerned. Most impartial observers agreed that the state had not even come close to placing Robert Welch at the scene of Gibson's murder. And it is likely, whatever the merits of the scientific evidence at Carpenter's trial, that its bulk and abstruseness ultimately confused and even irritated his jury.

So who killed Orville Gibson, barring the implausible idea that he tied himself up and leaped into the Connecticut River? Given the lapse of time—fifty years—the solution of his brutal murder now probably lies beyond the realm of possibility. Yet it is likely that there are still people alive, persons still living in Newbury and its surrounding towns, who know just what happened that awful New Year's Eve morning that took Orville Gibson's life. Rumors of deathbed confessions by the actual Gibson killers continue to abound—but it seems likely that those who know the truth will, like Gibson, take their secrets to the grave.

CHAPTER 6

"I AM INNOCENT!"

The Crime and Punishment of John P. Phair

D oes the state execute innocent persons? Is circumstantial evidence sufficient proof of guilt at a trial where a life is at stake? Can a condemned prisoner come within a hair of being executed, only to be saved by a last-minute reprieve? Such questions have lain at the heart of many a B movie and paperback melodrama. Cornell Woolrich's paranoid thriller *Phantom Lady* comes to mind: the nail-biting drama of an innocent man headed for the electric chair because no one can substantiate his valid alibi. But you don't have to plumb fiction and fantasy for such a scenario. It happened right here in Vermont, back in 1874 to a young man named John P. Phair. And if it didn't turn out the way anyone expected, well, blame reality, not the storyteller. Truth *is* stranger than fiction, as the tale of the Freese murder well illustrates.

It was June 9, 1874, a sunny day in Rutland, Vermont. The first wisps of smoke erupted from Ann Freese's house shortly before 6 AM. Few residents at her end of Forest Street thought much of it, as it could have come from her chimney or a backyard brushfire. By 6:30, however, smoke was pouring from all sides of her house, and alarmed spectators rushed to the scene. It was already too late. Three of Freese's neighbors, John Jardine, Abraham Whiting, and Charles McCarty, managed to get into the house and up the front stairs. From the landing Jardine could see Freese's body, lying on the bed in her bedroom. But the room was engulfed in flames, and the trio was steadily driven backward and out of the house as the fire inexorably consumed the entire structure. By the time firefighters arrived at 7 AM, there was nothing for anyone in the enormous crowd of spectators to do but watch it burn to the ground.

Two hours later a crew under the direction of Rutland poor overseer Franklin Billings began probing the ruins. Their search quickly turned into a murder-arson investigation. There wasn't much left of Ann Freese. Her corpse had fallen into the first-floor wreckage and was little more than a limbless torso and some bone fragments. But there was enough left of her for a thorough autopsy by local physicians Drs. Charles C. Allen and John A. Mead. Dentist Lewis T. Lawton soon confirmed her identity from a false tooth he had planted in her upper jaw, and the postmortem indicated that she had bled to death before the fire started. A deep five-inch gash showed that someone had cut her throat, severing her windpipe and several vital arteries. And a thorough sifting of the fire debris suggested that that same someone had also removed the treasure of cash, jewelry, silver plate, and other valuables Ann Freese was known to keep in her house.

The Rutland authorities didn't have far to look for a suspect— and they didn't look very far. It was an open secret in Rutland that Freese, who was a widow, had for some time been using her home as a brothel. Several young ladies, among them a soiled dove named Dora Wilson, had pursued their horizontal labors there, and it was rumored that many a prominent and married Rutland male was to be found of an evening climbing the sinful stairs of 92 Forest

Street. Lately, however, Ann herself had been seen almost exclusively in the company of John P. Phair, sometime machinist and recent emigrant from Vergennes. Phair's close association with the dubious Freese was the least of his attractions as a plausible suspect: He was also an ex-convict with a known penchant for robbery and personal violence. Worse yet, he had reportedly disappeared from Rutland the morning of Freese's death. The hue and cry for Phair was immediately broadcast throughout New England, and the Rutland selectmen offered a reward of $2,500 for the capture and conviction of Freese's killer.

Sometime that same afternoon, a train from Rutland arrived in Boston. One of its passengers disembarked and went to the Adams House Hotel. Signing in as "E. F. Smith, St. Albans, Vermont," he then proceeded to the pawnshop of Meyer Abraham at eighteen Salem Street. Claiming he was "dead broke," "Smith" proffered a watch and chain, beseeching Abraham to give him $40, which he needed to travel home. After dickering awhile, the man accepted $35 from Abraham and signed the pawn register, again as E. F. Smith. He then returned to the Adams House and spent the night in room 61. Departing the hotel in the morning, Smith subsequently visited several more pawnshops, attempting to pawn or sell a pair of opera glasses, a fine silken shawl, a worsted paisley shawl, and three rings. He easily disposed of the opera glasses and shawl, pawning them for $10 at the shop of James G. Pierce at 25 Howard Street. Before departing, he was also seen by Pierce's clerk John Haney and by fellow pawnbroker Morris Livingston.

A few minutes later E. F. Smith entered J. C. H. Voigt's jewelry store on Lagrange Street. Producing a Masonic ring, a woman's chased ring, and an onyx ring, he offered them to Voigt for $5. The suspicious Voigt refused to purchase them, and Smith left. Minutes later, he approached Samuel Erlich in his shop on Washington

Street and sold the rings outright for $5. Smith departed and was seen no more, except for one additional brief sighting by James Pierce at Court and Howard Streets in downtown Boston. Espying Smith on the street, Pierce turned to an acquaintance, pawnbroker Isaac Smith, and queried him as to whether he thought Smith looked like a "sharper." Isaac Smith replied, "If he is a sharper, he must be from Maine or Vermont, as they are the worst kind of sharpers." Sometime that same day Adams House porter James Doran found a shawl in room 61, apparently left there by E. F. Smith. It was a shabby item, inexpensively made and badly stained near one of its edges. But it would loom large in the fate of John P. Phair, for like the opera glasses, paisley shawl, watch, chain, and the three rings, it had quite recently belonged to Ann Freese.

The Rutland dragnet caught up with the missing Phair the following day. At one o'clock that morning, Rutland police officers N. S. Stearns and George W. Crawford arrested him on a Vergennes-bound passenger train in Cuttingsville, a whistle-stop some ten miles southeast of Rutland. Insisting at first he didn't even know about the murder, Phair soon confessed to the officers that someone had told him about it on the train. But he stoutly maintained his complete innocence, even after they took him off in handcuffs at Rutland and marched him to the jail. A thorough search disclosed no bloodstains on his clothing or any suspicious possessions; nor was there any trace of the ample wad of cash allegedly carried on the person of Mrs. Freese.

The noose closing fast on Phair's neck was soon considerably tightened by officers Crawford and Stearns. All the evidence suggested that Phair had traveled to Boston and that he had disposed of Freese's valuables there. Arriving in Boston that Friday, the two officers quickly hooked up with Boston police detective Benjamin Gould. Armed with a description of the missing valuables, they hit pay dirt on Saturday morning at Meyer Abraham's shop. Recalling the watch they described, Abraham hauled it out of his safe and read out its telltale serial number, 56375. Abraham also remembered that the watch pawner had mentioned he was staying at the Adams House, where Crawford and Stearns later talked to night clerk John Donovan Jr. Shown a jail photograph of Phair, Donovan identified him as E. F. Smith. Donovan also produced the shawl found in Smith's room, the stained garment so well known to Freese's acquaintances. More visits to pawnshops and jewelers turned up Freese's three rings, the opera glasses, and the worsted paisley shawl. Crawford and Stearns also turned up more witnesses willing and able to identify E. F. Smith as John P. Phair. Many of them did so at the inquest conducted by Justice Martin G. Everts, and Phair was forthwith indicted for the murder of Ann Freese and his trial set for the September court term. Citing the difficulties involved in proving the indigent Phair's alibi and acute public hostility to him in the Rutland area, his court-assigned counsel, lawyers Walter C. Dunton and W. G. Veazey, requested both a change of venue and a delay in his trial. Rutland Superior Court judge Hoyt H. Wheeler brushed their objections aside, insisting Rutland jurors could render a just verdict and that the testimony of witnesses should be heard while it was relatively fresh in their minds.

Who were these two persons hurtled from obscurity by the tragedy of this small-town murder? Little is known of Ann Freese, save the ghastly facts of her demise. Perhaps twenty-seven years old, this rather homely widow of hotel porter Alvin Freese had sunk into abject poverty after his death in 1868. But in a few years she had transformed her modest dwelling on Rutland's outskirts into the "Forest Street Young Ladies Social Club," better known to the town's discriminating and unchaste males as its most popular brothel. And whatever the sneers of Rutland's more upright folk,

Freese had apparently prospered, acquiring expensive jewelry, costly raiment, and frequently flashing the impressive wad of cash she carried on her person.

John P. Phair was a better-known quantity—and little of it seemed good. The son of a respectable Vergennes woolen manufacturer and his pious wife, John had proved a seeming "bad seed" from his birth in 1845. By adolescence he was already the terror of the Phair neighbors, many of whom avoided crossing the bridge by his parents' home for fear of encountering the bullying youth. Before reaching adulthood, he was already suspected of two attempted murders and several abortive robberies. Gloomy neighborhood prognostications about him proved true in 1865, when he was convicted of stealing some leather hides and sentenced to six years' hard labor in Windsor Prison. In 1871, in response to his parents' pleas and an alleged religious conversion, Phair was pardoned by Governor George W. Hendee. Returning to Vergennes, Phair initially seemed a reformed character, professing abhorrence for alcohol, bad companions, and idleness. Perhaps he was—but his personal redemption abruptly ceased upon his arrival in Rutland in April 1874. Finding work at the Mansfield & Stimson machine shop, he quickly made himself notorious as a profligate if unimaginative rake, drinking heavily, boasting of sexual conquests, and spending much of his leisure time at the Freese bordello. To the consternation of Phair and his lawyers, all the defects of his personal history were repeatedly ventilated and often embellished in the Rutland newspapers in the weeks before his trial.

That ordeal commenced on the morning of September 29. Though he was nominally still represented by Dunton and Veazey, Phair's defense was badly handicapped when Dunton fell ill and was replaced by neophyte lawyer David E. Nicholson halfway through the trial. Not that even Shakespeare's Portia might have saved

Phair: The case mounted against him by state's attorney Ebenezer J. Ormsbee and his assistants Charles Joyce and Martin Everts was devastating. Fifty-three witnesses appeared for the state, and almost all of them contributed to the fatal circumstantial evidence against Phair. After physicians Mead and Allen testified that the corpse found at 92 Forest Street was that of Ann Freese, a parade of witnesses told the jury that the "E. F. Smith" they had encountered in Boston on June 9 and 10, 1874, was John P. Phair. All of them, except an uncertain John Donovan Jr. of the Adams House, swore that Phair was the man who had spent the night there and disposed of the possessions of the murdered procuress. The prosecution argued less persuasively that Phair was lying about his whereabouts from the evening of Saturday, June 6, until June 9, the morning of the fire. They claimed that he had spent the intervening nights at Freese's house, rather than at the Berwick House hotel in Rutland. But while they were able to establish doubt that he had in fact slept at the hotel—the hotel's staff testifying that his bed linen remained undisturbed—they could not produce a witness who had actually seen him with Freese after June 6.

The state was more successful in its efforts to undermine Phair's alibi covering the interval between the probable time of the murder and his arrest at Cuttingsville. As he had since the time of his arrest, Phair claimed that he had arrived in Boston at 2:15 PM and immediately engaged a carriage to take him to another station, where he boarded a train for Providence, Rhode Island. His goal was to seek work at the American Screw Factory there, and after dining at a cheap restaurant near the Providence train station, he spent the night at an adjoining lodging house. The next morning, after discovering there was no work for him in Providence, he had taken the train back to Boston and thence to his foul destiny in Cuttingsville. True, he had lied about not knowing about Freese's murder before his arrest—but that prevarication hardly affected his alibi that he had been either en route to or in Providence at the time E. F. Smith was disposing of the murder loot. But Phair himself did not testify in his own behalf, and his lawyers could not produce a single witness who could corroborate any detail of his Providence alibi, save for a Mr. and Mrs. Stewart, who had ridden in his carriage as he traveled between the Boston railway stations. But no one could be found who had seen him on the Providence train, and no such lodging house or restaurant as he described could be found. And how was it that a man who allegedly doted on his Providence-dwelling sister had not even notified her that he was in that city on June 9 and 10, 1874? Having effectively impeached Phair's version of his movements, the state amplified its identification of John P. Phair and E. F. Smith with six expert handwriting witnesses, all of whom told the jury that the writing in the Adams House guest register, the Boston pawn tickets, and Phair's authenticated autograph were by the same hand.

Defeated in their efforts to validate Phair's alibi, Veazey and Nicholson concentrated their legal fire on the gaps in the prosecution's murder chronology. How, they argued, could Phair have murdered Freese, set the fire, and yet still have left Rutland on the 4:30 AM train? That was easy, the confident Ormsbee explained: Phair had cleverly heaped clothes on the corpse before setting the bed afire, successfully calculating that they would keep the fire quietly smoldering for several hours while he made his getaway. And why, Ormsbee continued, had Phair lied about being in Brandon, Vermont, on the day and night before Freese's murder? The evidence at his Rutland hotel was that Phair had not spent the night there, and his claim that he had slept the night of June 8 at the Brandon House Hotel in Brandon was denied in court by its proprietor, Riley Deming. Moreover, Phair claimed to have purchased a new shirt in Brandon on June 8, a type of shirt not ever sold there. Phair's motive in lying about his whereabouts before the murder, Ormsbee concluded for the jury's benefit, could only be that he must have spent that interval in the company of his victim. Indeed, the only time period that Phair could convincingly account for was his presence on the June 9 train to Boston—the very same train the Freese killer must have taken to enable him to start disposing of his murder loot there that same afternoon.

Given the overwhelming circumstantial evidence against their client, there were few factual matters for Nicholson and Veazey to dispute in their final arguments to the jury. So they concentrated on name-calling and character assassination. Further blackening the already sooty name of the murder victim, Nicholson heaped additional insults on her sordid memory: "I do not say that the town was honored by the murder, but it certainly was benefited by being rid of a being who was a disgrace to the better half of creation and a means of destroying the other half."

After castigating the police witnesses against Phair as greedy reward-seekers, Nicholson and Veazey offered equally vituperative slurs for the Boston pawnbrokers who had testified so damningly that John P. Phair was E. F. Smith: "The witnesses for this matter are Jew pawnbrokers," the defense argued, "and you all know what that means: Every one of these Jews do not claim that his oath has any sanctity except when administered by a rabbi."

Stretching the jury's credulity perhaps a bit too far, Nicholson suggested that the state had not even proved that Ann Freese was murdered—that her identifying denture may indeed have been a "false tooth" that belonged to someone else.

Veazey and Nicholson's impressive arsenal of abuse was not enough. After Judge Wheeler carefully charged the jury, the twelve men retired to consider their verdict at 7:50 PM on Saturday,

October 3, the fifth day of the trial. Three hours and forty-two minutes later they returned with a verdict of guilty to murder in the first degree, and Phair was speedily sentenced to die on the scaffold of Windsor Prison on the first Friday of April 1877. As prescribed by Vermont law, that generous interval would allow Phair to petition the Vermont legislature for a commutation of his death sentence. Although he later blamed his lawyers, Phair himself chose not to petition the legislature but placed all his hopes in Veazey and Nicholson's plea to the Vermont Supreme Court for a new trial. On February 4, 1875, the high court rejected all the defense exceptions, Justice Stephen Royce opining that even if all the defense objections to Phair's original trial had been granted, the verdict would have been the same. Chief Justice John Pierpoint then resentenced Phair to hang on the first Friday of April 1877.

Several days before his scheduled execution, Phair released his deathbed statement to the newspapers. Over eight thousand words in length, the document was a remarkable compound of self-pitying sanctimony and venomous accusation. Insisting on his innocence and accusing the Vermont newspapers of hopelessly prejudicing his jurors, Phair charged that he had been deliberately framed by Rutland police officers Stearns and Crawford in their perjured quest for the reward money. Spouting anti-Semitic slurs against the pawnbrokers who had testified against him, Phair also avowed a newfound (again!) religious faith. His profession of a pious Christianity did not prevent him from casting additional aspersions on the late Mrs. Freese. Indeed, he disclosed that she drank frequently, was altogether a woman of "very easy virtue" and, alas, a female wont to uttering oaths that made his "hair stand on end." What Phair's dying apologia did not include, however, was a convincing alibi for his whereabouts on June 9 and 10, 1874.

It was a very close call. The gallows was ready, the hangman's noose properly adjusted, a rosewood casket with silver trimmings sat in discreet proximity, and the audience of fifty spectators was in place a good half hour before Phair's scheduled demise at 2 PM, April 6, 1877. But at 1:36 PM, just before Windsor County sheriff Sony W. Stimson arrived at Phair's cell for the final walk, a messenger handed Stimson a telegram from Vermont governor Horace Fairbanks. It contained a reprieve for Phair, halting his execution a mere twenty-four minutes before the dismal event. What had happened?

An astonished world soon learned how Phair's unlikely salvation had evolved out of an improbable combination of contingency and chance. At nine o'clock that very morning, Robert Lowhee, an employee of the American Novelty Company in Boston, had read the text of Phair's dying statement published in that morning's edition of the *Boston Herald*. Moved by Phair's anguished claim of innocence, Lowhee mentioned Phair's plight to his employer, Marshall D. Downing. Downing, in turn, was so struck by the story that he had Lowhee fetch him a copy of the *Herald*. Reading Phair's account of his trip from Providence to Boston on June 10, Downing suddenly recalled encountering and conversing with just such a man on *that very train on that very day at that very time*. Indeed, he remembered that the man had said he was a Vermont machinist and that he had unsuccessfully sought a job in Providence. Indeed, at the time Downing had so sympathized with the machinist that he had actually offered him a job at his firm. He had forgotten all about it—and now it seemed he had a chance to save the poor wretch's life. By noon that day Downing got off a telegram to Vermont governor Fairbanks, which finally caught up with him at St. Johnsbury, where Fairbanks was able to wire Sheriff Stimson just in time to halt Phair's execution. A second reprieve extended Phair's respite from the gallows until at least April 4, 1879.

It seemed too good to be true—and it was. Despite ample time and opportunity, Phair and his counsel were unable to prove Downing's assertions. Phair was not even personally confronted with Downing until April 2, 1879, and their supposed mutual recognition appeared suspiciously disingenuous to its official witnesses. Following an additional reprieve, Vermont Supreme Court justices H. Henry Ross and Jonathan Powers rejected Phair's final appeal on April 9, ruling that Downing's suspect identification of Phair—a man he had seen briefly almost five years before—was far outweighed by the testimony of the Boston pawnbrokers that Phair was the vendor of Ann Freese's valuables. Rubbing it in, Justice Powers stated that he had now heard the evidence against Phair three times and was more convinced than ever that he was Ann Freese's killer.

Governor Fairbanks's original reprieve had been greeted with sighs of relief and public shuddering at how close the state had come to killing an innocent man on the basis of mere circumstantial evidence. But the ultimate failure of Phair's alibi and constant newspaper reiteration of the evidence against him eventually diminished the ranks of Phair's defenders to the tiny remnant of those purists opposed to any capital punishment.

As with Shakespeare's Thane of Cawdor, nothing in John Phair's life so became him like the leaving of it. His last reprieve expiring, he walked calmly to the Windsor Prison gallows as sixty spectators gawked on April 10, 1879. Permitted to make a final statement, he eschewed his usual recriminations and simply stated for the last time, "I am innocent!" He remained calm and silent as Sheriff Stimson read the death warrant, a contracted brow the only sign of his turmoil. After his arms and legs were pinioned, Deputy Sheriff Rollin Amsden made the final adjustment of the rope to Phair's neck. One observer noted that it was the same rope used to hang several previous criminals and the very same noose prepared for Phair in 1877. Phair barely had time to mutter, "Lord, remember me! Lord, remember me!" before Stimson sprang the trap at 2:11 PM. With a dull thud, Phair fell six feet and, as the fall did not break his neck, strangled to death for several minutes in front of his horrified audience. Whatever his guilt—which seems incontestable —he died still protesting his innocence of the murder of Ann Freese. In accordance with his last request, his remains were shipped to his mother in Vergennes, on a midnight train deliberately rerouted so his casket would not pass through Rutland.

POSTSCRIPT

Shortly after the original version of this tale appeared in *Vermont Sunday Magazine* in 2006, several great-grandchildren of John Phair's sister Mary shared an intriguing epilogue to the Phair narrative in a letter to the *Barre Montpelier Times Argus*. In it they recalled a story told to Mary's son Henry—their father—when he was young. This family anecdote was that some years after John Phair was hanged, his mother was contacted by a Vermont priest. The unidentified priest told her that he heard a recent confession from a dying man, in which the man had admitted killing Ann Freese and begged the priest to tell Phair's family. This startling anecdote may be true, although the author has encountered a remarkable number of similar family oral traditions, all of which invariably conclude with the exoneration of a seemingly deep-dyed and arrant villain.

CHAPTER 7

"THE BEST OF A BAD BUSINESS"

Vermont's Greatest Manhunt: The Elizabeth Weatherup Murder

Vermont's ongoing struggle with the possibility that murderer Donald Fell may be put to death resonates with historic echoes from the state's last executions—the electrocutions of Francis Blair and Donald Demag in 1954 for the murder of Elizabeth Weatherup. The debate over the killers' mental states especially anticipated the focus on Fell's dismal childhood and capacity for controlling his actions. Whatever one's convictions about capital punishment, the Weatherup murder and its social context provide a fascinating glimpse into how such matters were perceived by Vermonters of a half century past.

———

It must have seemed like a scene from a prison melodrama like *The Shawshank Redemption* or *The Big House*. But it wasn't Tim Robbins or Robert Montgomery—and it surely wasn't a peaceful movie set. It was Vermont's Windsor Prison, and it was Wednesday, July 30, 1952. Shortly after 7 AM, two convicts prepared for their daily work detail in the prison yard. One was Francis Blair, at thirty-one years old a career criminal serving the latest of his numerous and multi-state prison stints, a seven-to-ten-year term for grand larceny and burglary. The other was Donald Demag, twenty-nine, a "lifer" doing time for the brutal 1948 slaying of a Burlington harness maker. Things happened fast that fateful morning. As Blair passed by a prison work truck, he noticed the key in the ignition. Seconds later, he and Demag vaulted into the truck's cab and Blair floored the ten-wheeled, eight-ton vehicle toward the massive prison gates. It was no contest: The speeding truck easily smashed through a ten-by-twelve-foot steel barrier, dragging it some distance before crunching through another steel gate to the outside and freedom. Before the astonished prison tower guards could even think of shooting, the truck was already careening south down U.S. Route 5. And Vermont's greatest manhunt was on—an episode that would climax in the brutal death of an innocent housewife and Vermont's last criminal executions.

It took startled Vermont authorities some time to mount an organized pursuit of the two convicts. But they got a welcome break only forty-five minutes after the escape, when the prison truck was found abandoned at the intersection of Routes 5 and 11, about twenty miles from the prison and close to the Cheshire Bridge connecting Springfield to Charlestown, New Hampshire. Vermont lawmen correctly surmised that the two fugitives had abandoned the truck when it ran out of gas and then fled into the densely wooded environs of Springfield. Aided by New Hampshire police, they set up roadblocks, procured bloodhounds from New Hampshire, brought in powerful searchlights, sent two Civil Air Patrol planes to search from the sky, and called for civilian volunteers to join what was already becoming an unprecedented manhunt.

In the aftermath of its tragic conclusion, there would be much second-guessing of the officials who directed the search for Demag and Blair. But it is difficult now to argue that they could have done better with the available resources. By nightfall that Wednesday there were at least thirty Vermont state troopers and local police officers combing the miles of woods and brush where the convicts were supposed—correctly—to be hiding. But the search area was very rough terrain, and the bloodhounds lost the trail of the convicts only a mile or so from the truck. More critically, there just weren't enough civilian volunteers to comb the many square miles where the two convicts might be hiding. Area residents became increasingly apprehensive as Wednesday faded into Thursday and then into Friday without a trace of the escapees, repeatedly described by lawmen as "dangerous." But whatever their private fears, Vermont authorities remained publicly confident about the unprecedentedly intense dragnet; the tone of their breezy assurance was best expressed by Windsor Prison associate warden Harry Ward, who stated his smug conviction that the two men were already despairing and reduced to "eating berries and stealing food from gardens."

Ward was right about the berries but badly mistaken about Demag and Blair's morale. After their repeated attempts to escape the Springfield region were foiled by the sight of police roadblocks, they holed up for a while in an empty estate guesthouse. Catching sight of an armed searcher Wednesday afternoon, they put their hands up and almost surrendered before realizing that they hadn't been seen. Two days later, they had a similar fright in the Goulds Mill area when a Vermont state trooper actually had them in the sight of his rifle, only to wave them off under the misimpression they were fellow sleuths.

The central tragedy of this epic manhunt developed just minutes after that second near-capture. Noticing the illumination coming from a nearby house, Demag and Blair hid themselves under cover of an earthen bank until the last light was extinguished. Shortly afterward the two men moved in, Blair armed with a three-foot piece of iron fence piping and Demag with an eight-inch steel file. Smashing the glass in a back door, the convicts forced their way into the kitchen and began a stumbling and frantic search in the dark for food and weapons.

The sound of the back-door glass breaking awakened Elizabeth Weatherup about midnight. The fifty-four-year-old housewife and community activist had returned from a civil defense meeting late that evening and joined her fifty-seven-year-old husband, Donald, who was already asleep in their second-floor bedroom. He was mostly deaf and hadn't heard the noise, but she immediately awakened him and began to dress while he went downstairs to investigate. Entering the darkened kitchen, he saw their Boston terrier by the back door. Thinking the dog was the source of the noise, he went to let it out the door. As he did so he was hit from behind with terrific force—a blow from Francis Blair's iron pipe that felled him. As he went down, however, he grappled with Blair, who hit him several more blows until he ceased resisting. It seems likely that Demag joined in at some point in the struggle, employing the sharp end of his file to inflict about a dozen ugly puncture wounds on Donald Weatherup's left arm, left wrist, and back.

As Donald Weatherup slumped to the floor, apparently unconscious, Elizabeth Weatherup confronted his two assailants. Screaming once or twice, she threw a teacup at Blair and ran toward an adjacent bathroom. Blair caught up with her there before she could lock the door and smashed her on the skull with his pipe. Falling onto the side of the bathtub, the stunned woman began pleading for mercy, begging that he not hit her again and sobbing, "I won't tell I saw you!" Her cries were useless: The pitiless Blair hit her at least four times altogether, inflicting multiple skull fractures before leaving her a moaning wreck, slumped over the side of the bathtub as her life's blood poured down the drain. Apparently Demag also joined in, stabbing the prostrate woman in the chest with his file. Leaving her to die, they returned to the kitchen to continue their search for booty. Unnerved by their own violence, they failed to notice that the man they had assaulted was no longer lying on the floor. A few minutes later, frightened by noises outside, they fled the house to seek safety in the woods.

Miraculously, Donald Weatherup had survived the beating that left him with severe lacerations of the scalp, face, and right hand, a fractured left wrist, a fractured rib, multiple puncture wounds, and a serious loss of blood. Regaining consciousness as the two convicts attacked his wife, he had feigned death until the men moved into another room. Painfully dragging his maimed body and leaving copious bloodstains in his wake, he managed to get through the kitchen and out the door. Finding himself unpursued, he crawled one hundred yards to the home of his neighbor, Raymond Lemire, and knocked on his door. Awakened by the summons, Lemire was initially reluctant to open his door to this blood-covered, apparent stranger, but eventually realized it was his neighbor, who despite his terrible injuries managed to croak out, "They've slugged me and they got my wife." Lemire brought him in, dressed his wounds, and called for a physician and the Springfield Police.

By the time Elizabeth Weatherup died of her injuries five hours later at 5:45 AM, many citizens in the vicinity were already aware of the tragedy and participating in the armed search for her killers. Police bloodhounds, led by champion sniffer "Dr. Watson," were brought to the Weatherup home. Smelling some bedsheets brought from the cells of the escaped prisoners, the dogs quickly picked up the trail leading back into the woods. By midmorning that Saturday there were as many as 250 armed men looking for the escapees, and the discovery of Demag's hat at 10:15 AM quickened the conviction that the ring around the fugitives was closing at last.

The end came about an hour later in a wooded area near the Frank Bishop farm by the Skitchewaug Trail. Like many of the Weatherups' Springfield neighbors, searcher Kenneth Plumb knew every inch of the local terrain, and he spotted the fugitives first, as they crouched hiding by a stone wall. He shouted his discovery to his brother Francis, a local dairy farmer. Firing his .300 caliber Savage rifle to alert nearby searchers, Francis hollered "Stop or I'll shoot!" as Demag and Blair scampered farther into the brush. Running in pursuit, Francis fired twice, Kenneth fired once, and they were soon joined by fellow searchers as they closed in on the fleeing killers. Suddenly, as in a feature film, a loudspeaker blared out the words the anxious posse had so long awaited: "Demag, Blair, you are entirely surrounded by law-enforcement agents. If you want to live, come out." Seconds later, Demag came streaking out of the brush. Vermont state trooper Marvin Pfenning fired once and, having missed, settled for a flying tackle, which brought Demag down. A minute later, surrounded by pursuers, Blair quietly surrendered, walking out of the woods and saying, "I give up." Haggard and handcuffed, the two prisoners were whisked away to the Springfield police station before the mood of the civilian posse got any uglier. The Weatherups were well known and well liked, and one armed eyewitness of Demag's capture gestured toward a towering tree and muttered to his neighbors, "There's the tree. Let's string him up." Noting that Blair had only been nicked in the finger by one of the shots fired at him, another observer regretted, "It's too bad we had to miss the _____ the way we did."

At the Springfield police station, Demag and Blair both made voluntary statements detailing their escape, the murder, and their capture. Demag was generally morose and silent in the wake of his capture, but Blair soon regained his habitual, verbose cockiness. Gloating that he and Demag would be "heroes" to their fellow inmates when they returned to Windsor Prison, he showed no remorse about the murder and bragged, "Next time we'll have you all over the place." Indeed, his only stated regret was that "We was out four days and never even had a glass of beer."

The official recriminations produced by the affair ultimately focused, quite properly, on the initial escape, rather than the more comprehensible delay in recapturing the two prisoners. Even before Governor Lee E. Emerson launched his official probe of the prison breakout, Vermont journalists had begun posing embarrassing questions to Windsor Prison warden John L. Ferguson and his staff. Such questions were most forcefully articulated in the *Springfield Reporter* in its editorial following the murder of Elizabeth Weatherup and the capture of her killers:

> Donald Demag, in addition to being a lifer and a convicted murderer, also had escaped previously from the prison. Why was this man, obviously a dangerous prisoner, permitted the freedom of the prison yard? . . . Why were the keys of the 10-wheel truck in which the prisoners made their get-away left in the ignition. . . . What was the matter with the guard on the wall of the prison, who was armed with a shotgun, that he didn't fire at the tires of the truck when the vehicle came hurling *[sic]* through the gates? Why did it take so long to get out the alarm? Springfield police did not receive a call to go into action until nearly a half-hour after the prisoners had broken through the gates.

The writer of that editorial, *Reporter* editor Gerald E. McLaughlin, concluded his scorching queries with a judgment of the accused killers that was shared by many Vermonters of his era: "Demag and Blair have proven that prisoners at bay are as dangerous as wild animals. And they should be tracked down and treated as such."

Although most of the questions raised by the handling of the escape and manhunt were never clearly answered, Governor Emerson's investigation did result in a tightening of Windsor Prison security and the punishment of its culpably lax officials. Warden Ferguson was suspended for sixty days, guard Roy Sweet for thirty days, and associate warden Ward was fired outright.

Meanwhile, the prosecution of Elizabeth Weatherup's killers went forward with a speed that present-day Vermonters might find astonishing. Indicted on charges of first-degree murder by a Windsor County grand jury on August 21, 1952, Blair and Demag were subsequently sent to the State Hospital for the Insane in Waterbury for observation. With authorities now painfully aware of the potential consequences of allowing the two convicts to be together, they were examined by psychiatrists there at different times.

Who were these two men, who now faced a mandatory death sentence on charges of first-degree murder? Francis Blair, the probable leader and dominant member of the duo, was the less complex of the two felons. Born in Barre about 1920, he was placed in a Burlington orphanage two years later after his mother, Margaret, was permanently committed to the State Hospital for the Insane in Waterbury. Some years later, entirely abandoned by his father, an allegedly unaffectionate ne'er-do-well, Blair ran away and lived with relatives in Orange County. From adolescence on, his work record as a casual laborer and truck driver was spotty, being frequently interrupted by prison or jail terms. Hardened prematurely between 1935 and 1952 into a career criminal and callous thug, he drifted through at least three state prison systems, serving time on various grand larceny and robbery charges. The year 1952 found him doing his seven-to-ten-year rap at Windsor Prison, and it was there that he met the malleable Donald Demag. He soon discovered that Demag had been planning an escape for some time, but their opportunity with the truck on July 30 came as a serendipitous surprise to both of them.

Demag's biography manifested a similar dreariness, if a greater uncertainty about his moral capacity. Born to a respectable Burlington couple, Donald contracted scarlet fever at the age of three, a wasting ordeal that put him in a coma for five weeks and left him largely deaf in his right ear. His mother would later testify that the illness changed his personality for the worse; it certainly also seemed related to the epileptic seizures from which he henceforth suffered. After an adolescent interval at a school for the deaf, Donald returned home, a restless and unhappy youth. Increasingly given to lying and stealing, he began his correctional career at the age of seventeen at the state's Weeks School for delinquent children. His next few years were sprinkled with convictions for hit-and-run driving and both petty and grand larceny.

Demag's life took an upturn in the mid-1940s, when he married his childhood sweetheart, Virginia. The couple had their first child in 1947, and by March of the next year Virginia was pregnant again. Then it all went bad in a few seconds of violence. Friendly with eighty-one-year-old Burlington harness maker Francis E. Racicot, the unemployed Donald had borrowed $30 from him. But when Demag returned to Racicot's shop at twenty-four Center Street on the afternoon of March 11, 1948, for another loan, the harness maker angrily refused and told him to leave. Aware that Racicot was reputed to carry large amounts of cash on his person, the enraged Demag forced him into a back room and bludgeoned him to death with a convenient stove shaker. Finding less than $100 in Racicot's wallet, he fled from the shop in terror.

Demag had good reason to be upset. He soon discovered from the newspapers that he had overlooked another wallet on Racicot's person that contained $500. Worse yet, an eyewitness had seen someone wearing a red cap and red coat leaving the murder scene. The apprehensive Demag quickly disposed of the incriminating scarlet coat and hat, hurling them on top of a nearby garage. But that act, too, was seen by an eyewitness, and before Demag knew it he was in police custody and signing a full confession. Against the advice of his attorney, Joseph Wool, he spurned an insanity plea and accepted a plea bargain of second-degree murder and a life sentence in Windsor Prison. Noting that psychiatrists at the Waterbury hospital believed that Demag sometimes suffered psychotic episodes, Wool blamed his client's childhood illness and an uncaring society for the Racicot murder, telling reporters, "[Demag] is one of the unfortunates for whom society must assume some blame. Unfortunately the state does not have facilities for handling such medical cases . . . the shame is as much ours as anyone else's."

Life in Windsor Prison did not improve Demag's disposition, and newcomer Francis Blair was doubtless impressed with the surly demeanor of the powerfully built problem prisoner when he encountered him in 1952. Blair was probably also impressed with the story of Demag's prior prison escape. Leaving a crude dummy in his bed, Demag had taken a fourteen-foot sign from a prison shop and used it to scale the prison wall on July 27, 1950. Admittedly, his follow-through was not so impressive. Three days later, after wandering aimlessly as far as Montreal and back, he was picked up in Derby Line by alert immigration policeman J. J. Fell. Unable to articulate a coherent story, Demag soon confessed his identity and was returned to Windsor Prison with an additional punitive term tacked onto his life sentence. He might have spent the rest of his life there, in all likelihood a chronically uncooperative and problem prisoner. But then, in early 1952, he met Windsor Prison newcomer Francis Blair.

For reasons unknown, Vermont attorney general Elliott F.

Barber Jr. decided to try Blair and Demag separately. Blair's trial got under way on March 16, 1953, with Barber and Windsor County state's attorney Lewis E. Springer Jr. prosecuting, Joseph O'Neill defending Blair, and Judge Paul A. Chase presiding. As Blair's basic plea was not guilty by reason of insanity, the trial's early days were a straightforward and uncontested presentation of the grisly facts of Elizabeth Weatherup's murder.

The first of the trial's two key contests came at the end of the March 18 afternoon session. After dismissing the jury from the courtroom, Judge Chase listened as the four attorneys battled over the admissibility of two explicit and detailed confessions made and signed by Blair on August 2 and August 4, 1952. After more argument the next morning, Chase ruled them admissible, and Barber read them aloud to the jury of five men and seven women. O'Neill had done well to so strenuously oppose their admission, for Blair's callous confessions left no doubt about his guilt or feral disposition.

The second and even more crucial battle came early in the trial's second week. O'Neill was banking heavily on Blair's insanity plea, telling the jury in his opening statement that even if Blair "might have known the consequences of his act, he was the victim of impulse, and even that if he knew the wrong of his act, that he could not resist." To support such contentions, he put officials from the Windsor Prison staff on the stand to tell stories of Blair's allegedly bizarre prison behavior. Such tales included Blair's repeated assertions that unidentified "enemies" were trying to kill him by putting glass in his food, and that there was sometimes a mysterious woman in his cell, sometimes "a little man." The tenor of the insanity testimony intensified with the appearance of Brandon psychiatrist Dr. Frederick C. Thorne on March 23. Thorne had interviewed Blair several times, and he now recounted the prisoner's chilling statements for the jury. They included his recollected joy of killing Elizabeth Weatherup ("I was thinking how nice it was to see blood and hear her howl. It made me feel good inside") and his bleakly simple code of ethics ("What I do is right, and what I do is law"). Dr. Thorne then stated his opinion that Blair was a "psychopathic personality with psychosis" who could neither tell right from wrong nor control his "irresistible" impulses. O'Neill next read into the record a deposition by Ohio prison psychiatrist Dr. E. Stanley Anderson. In 1945 Anderson had examined Blair at Lima State Hospital, an Ohio prison for the insane. His current opinion was that Blair had been insane in 1945.

O'Neill's strenuous efforts to play the insanity card failed utterly. Anderson's deposition was countered by depositions from other Ohio prison psychiatrists, who derided his 1945 diagnosis and suggested Blair had been feigning mental illness at the time. And Thorne's conclusion that Blair was insane was met by the rebuttal testimony of Dr. J. H. P. Forrest, a psychiatrist at the Waterbury hospital. He had examined Blair there, and he now accused Blair of pretending to be insane. When O'Neill imprudently asked what Forrest thought Blair had to gain by such a pretense, the doctor bluntly replied, "The difference between life and the electric chair." Dr. Rupert Chittick, the director of the Waterbury hospital, followed Forrest, further damaging Blair's defense with his statement that Blair was "sane and not mentally ill."

The case went to the jury on Saturday, March 28, 1953. Given Blair's admission that he had killed Elizabeth Weatherup, Judge Chase carefully explained to the jurors that the only possible verdicts were guilty of first-degree murder or not guilty by reason of insanity. The twelve jurors took only two and a half hours to find Blair guilty, a verdict that he took with his usual blasé insouciance.

After asking O'Neill if he could sit down, he queried, "When do they burn me?"

Donald Demag's trial in December 1953 was a near carbon-copy reprise of the Blair trial. With Judge Albert W. Barney presiding and Elliott Barber again prosecuting, Demag was again defended by Burlington attorney Joseph Wool. As expected, Wool concentrated on proving Demag insane and trying to exclude his written confessions from the record. But after hearing arguments, Judge Barney ruled the confessions admissible. And Wool also failed to present a plausible insanity defense, despite putting Demag's parents and ex-wife on the stand to expound the doleful details of his childhood illnesses and youthful delinquency. His relatives were followed by Windsor Prison officials who described Demag's frequently bizarre prison antics and three clumsy suicide attempts. Dr. Forrest resurfaced to opine that although Demag had suffered bouts of temporary insanity, the fact that he so clearly remembered the details of his escape and the murder indicated that he was sane at the time those events occurred. Perhaps Forrest's most interesting disclosure was that Demag's intelligence tests showed an IQ score ranging from a low eighty-eight to a dismal seventy-one. Then Dr. Chittick took the stand to support Forrest's contention that Demag was sane and knew right from wrong at the time of the murder.

The trial's only real excitement came on December 16, its eighth day, when Francis Blair was brought to the courthouse to testify. A dubious Judge Barney immediately dismissed the jury and held a hearing to determine Blair's competence as a witness. The hearing was soon aborted when Wool suddenly withdrew Blair as a defense witness, apparently after evidence surfaced that Blair and Demag had contrived a false alibi to the effect that Demag had been incapacitated by an epileptic fit while Blair was killing Elizabeth Weatherup.

It took Demag's jury of eight men and four women just over four hours to pronounce him guilty of first-degree murder on December 19, 1953.

Blair's appeal had been denied by the Vermont Supreme Court in October, and Governor Emerson refused to grant clemency. To his credit, the hitherto apparently conscienceless Blair mellowed somewhat in his final days, confessing his guilt in a letter to the governor and pleading that his accomplice be spared. He went to his death calmly on February 8, 1954, whispering the rosary with prison chaplain Father William Ready as the two-thousand-volt shock hit him in the electric chair. Pronounced dead at 10:15 PM, he was buried in the prison yard, and Father Ready assured reporters that Blair died "a reconciled sinner."

Demag's demise meticulously duplicated the details of Blair's final days. After his appeals to the Vermont Supreme Court and Governor Emerson failed, he resigned himself to his fate and accepted both Father Ready's spiritual consolations and the more mundane pleasures of a final repast of pork chops, a baked potato, chocolate milk, chocolate cake, and chocolate ice cream. He, too, was mumbling a Hail Mary as he died in the electric chair on the night of December 8, 1954, and he, too, was buried in the Windsor Prison yard.

In marked contrast to the current era, there was no public protest and little sympathy for the condemned generated by the Blair and Demag executions, the only two Vermont electrocutions to occur within a single year. (There were three hangings in 1879 and two hangings in both 1864 and 1881.) Most Vermonters thought the two killers had it coming, and the *Springfield Reporter* bluntly summarized local feeling about the condemned killers two days after Blair's execution:

> There was no one in Springfield who regretted that Blair was to die. They remembered kindly Elizabeth Weatherup and felt it was the best of a bad business that the ones who attacked her should die. . . . Springfield's reaction could be summed up in the words of a prison guard, who, after the execution, was quoted as saying, "Well, that's that."

CHAPTER 8

A VERY DARROW ESCAPE

The 1926 Cecelia Gullivan Murder

Whatever its abstract morality, the history of capital punishment in America strongly suggests that its application has often been arbitrary, if not downright capricious. This has been true even in relatively Edenic Vermont, notwithstanding its comparative scarcity of capital cases. For every one of the twenty-five killers executed in the Green Mountain State, one can easily identify comparable slayers who, despite their demonic acts, somehow eluded the gallows or electric chair. And no case better illustrates this contention than the remarkable saga of John C. Winters, spared at the eleventh hour by the intervention of America's greatest defense attorney: Clarence Darrow.

Darrow's champions might well have had Winters in mind when they christened the legendary lawyer "The Attorney for the Damned." By all available evidence, Winters was a repulsive brute. A hardened thug practically from the cradle, he earned his first jail stint at fifteen and by the age of twenty-one had logged two prison terms. His offenses included an assault with a bottle on a companion during a drinking binge, and a sexual attack on a young girl. The year of 1926 found him in an interval of apparent stability. Married and the father of two young children, Winters worked as a machinist for a Windsor manufacturing company. Or at least he did until Saturday, November 6. Within twenty-four hours, Windsor would be in turmoil, an innocent woman would be dead in her bed, and Winters would be traveling the fast track to Vermont's electric chair.

Bessie Pandjiris knew something was amiss when she awoke in bed, shortly before 2 AM that Sunday morning. A middle-aged nurse, Mrs. Pandjiris resided at 7 Main Street, the home of Miss Margaret Evarts, a wealthy invalid under her professional care. Awakened by a loud noise, Pandjiris switched on her bedside light, only to find a rough-looking man wearing a brown overcoat and a dark sweater by the side of her bed. His first words were a demand for money and jewelry, which she begged him to take, if only he would spare her life. Ignoring her plea, he suddenly and viciously attacked her, gouging her eyes with his fingers, pulling her by the hair, and knocking her to the floor with repeated blows and with the unmistakable intention of a sexual assault. But Pandjiris's cries and the noise of the scuffle alerted two other women in adjacent bedrooms, and as they appeared in the doorway, Pandjiris's assailant jumped up and ran out of the house into the night. He left behind a badly bruised, terrified woman—and a substantial quantity of burrs, seeds, sand, and dirt on the bed and floor of Pandjiris's room.

Soon apprised of the attack on Pandjiris, Windsor lawmen did what they could. But Chief of Police Michael Degnan and Windsor County sheriff Wallis Fairbanks initially had little to go on, save the traces of soil and Pandjiris's insistence that her attacker's face had seemed familiar. Twenty-four hours of calming rest considerably refreshed the nurse's memory, and by Monday morning the Windsor authorities were looking for the man she had identified:

local resident and known ex-convict John C. Winters. But by the time they came for him at his home that afternoon, he was wanted not only as the Pandjiris attack suspect but as the perpetrator of the most shocking murder in Windsor County history.

Cecelia Gullivan, forty-four, was a woman of personal charm, admirable character, and inflexibly predictable habits. So when she didn't show up for her work as treasurer of the Cone Automatic Machine Company that Monday morning, her boss Frank S. Cone immediately surmised something was wrong. Going to her bungalow, he found it unlocked and walked in. He soon discovered Cecelia lying in her bed on a sleeping porch and, unable to rouse her, called in her personal physician, Dr. Stoddard Martin. Quickly determining that she was dead and that her corpse showed evidence of violence, Martin in turn called in Chief Degnan and Sheriff Fairbanks. Their examination of the premises suggested that robbery had not been the motive in the fatal assault, as the house had not been ransacked and the intruder had ignored a clearly visible pocketbook and a diamond ring. More interestingly, Degnan and Fairbanks found traces of sand, seeds, dirt, and burrs on the victim's bed linen. Apparently left behind by her killer, the detritus was identical to that found in Bessie Pandjiris's bedroom. The autopsy on Gullivan's corpse, performed on Monday evening by Dr. William Kent, the state pathologist, indicated that she had been beaten to death and that her intruder had struck sometime early Sunday morning, probably shortly after the assault on Pandjiris.

The net of incrimination soon closed on Winters. Immediately incarcerated in a death-row cell at Windsor Prison, he was confronted with Bessie Pandjiris on the evening of Tuesday, November 11. Although he denied any knowledge of either the assault on her or the murder of Cecelia Gullivan, he became so overwrought as to exclaim, "I hope that I may die! I hope that I may hang! I hope to be shot." Recovering from this spasm of hysteria, he muttered, "If I did it, I don't remember it."

With the exception of Pandjiris's identification, the case against Winters remained circumstantial, then and forever. Investigators were able to trace the movements of Gullivan's killer with convincing accuracy. Removing a window from her cellar, he had dropped into a coal bin. He then climbed the stairs to the first floor and walked through the living room onto the sleeping porch, where he attacked Gullivan—most probably with a two-inch-wide chisel and a piece of an automobile suspension spring, implements that were found hidden in Winters's home when police arrested him. Standing up on the bed and astride Gullivan, the killer had left clear traces of his coal-smudged footprints on the bedsheets as he delivered a series of fatal blows to Gullivan's neck and head. Afterward, he had fled from the house toward an adjacent millpond with a dam. Throwing the only two items he had taken from Gullivan's house—a bloody pillow and pillowcase—into the pond, he then fled across the dam and through a barbed-wire fence, most likely in a direct path to the home of John C. Winters. And when Winters was taken into custody a day later, the cuffs of his pants were found to contain burrs, sand, and dirt identical to the matter found in the Pandjiris and Gullivan bedrooms. With the discovery of bloodstains on his clothing and scratches on his legs—most likely souvenirs of his passage through the barbed wire—the evidence against Winters seemed complete. Public feeling against Winters, already intense, was further inflamed by newspaper reports that he had recently made unwelcome sexual advances to at least one other woman and that Cecelia Gullivan's mother had suffered a heart attack when she saw her daughter's mutilated corpse.

Our ancestors may have sometimes denied justice, but they

certainly didn't much delay it. On December 16, 1926, just five weeks after his arrest, Winters was indicted by a Windsor County grand jury for the murder of Gullivan and the assault on Pandjiris. Five weeks later, his trial opened before Judge Frank D. Thompson, assisted by Judges William S. Dana and Burton M. Newton. Prosecuting the case were Vermont attorney general J. Ward Carver, special deputy attorney Raymond Trainor, and Windsor County state's attorney Robert Twitchell. Defending Winters were attorneys Herbert G. Tupper of Springfield and Fred Bicknell of Windsor.

If lacking, perhaps, in legal rigor, the Winters trial was not destitute of memorable theatrics. Not content with their impressive arsenal of circumstantial evidence, the prosecutors from the outset of the trial labored mightily—and successfully—to meld the Pandjiris and Gullivan assaults, both with respect to perpetrator and motive. The evidence was convincing that Pandjiris's assailant, positively identified by her as Winters, had been motivated by a "lustful purpose," rather than robbery. If the prosecutors, after airing the sickening details of Panjiris's nightmarish ordeal, could convince the jury that Gullivan's attacker was motivated by that same unspeakable lustful purpose, then it would not be difficult to convince them that the same man was responsible for both crimes.

J. Ward Carver and his assistants built their case against Winters methodically. Dr. William Kent told the jury the details of his autopsy, emphasizing the violence inflicted on Cecelia Gullivan and the telltale evidence of burrs, sand, and smudgy footprints left by her attacker on her bedsheets. Kent was followed by Windsor County lawmen, who testified about the discovery of Gullivan's murder and the evidence found on Winters's clothing and at the scenes of the two assaults. That evidence, particularly the burrs, sand, dirt, and coal dust, were then analyzed and explained to the jury by state pathologist Charles F. Whitney. Whitney's emphatic conclusion that the material found on Winters's clothing was identical to the detritus found at the assault scenes was dramatically amplified by having several microscopes brought into the courtroom so the jury members could validate Whitney's assertions with their own eyes.

After delays occasioned by the illness of several jurors and defense attorney Tupper, the state's case turned to what might be termed its "shock and awe" phase on Wednesday, January 26. Standing in front of the jury, Dr. Kent displayed to them the severed head of Cecelia Gullivan, which he had removed during the autopsy, while he calmly explained the nature of its injuries. As John Winters looked on impassively, chewing gum, Kent placed the defendant's chisel into the various wounds and demonstrated their perfect correspondence with the probable murder weapon. Yet that shocking exhibition was only prelude to the show on Friday afternoon, January 28. Under the direction of Sheriff Fairbanks, the Gullivan murder scene was re-created in the courtroom for the jury, as deputies replicated her sleeping porch, complete with bed, linens, an alarm clock, and the dead woman's slippers. Although this dramatic exhibit furnished no new circumstantial evidence, it afforded the prosecution another opportunity to let Dr. Kent testify, over strenuous defense objections, that the dual smudges on Gullivan's bed linens were very likely the footprints of her killer.

The remainder of the state's case against Winters was devoted to delineating his motives and destroying his alibi. The latter task was an easy one, particularly as Winters's insistence that he was too drunk to remember most of the murder night hardly aided his lawyers in constructing an exculpatory timetable for their client. Winters claimed to have imbibed several pints or quarts of wine and "white mule" on the murder night. But while numerous witnesses could testify to his copious drinking that night, none of them would swear that he was significantly impaired by his imbibing. And his claim that he had driven six miles to Hartland Four Corners at midnight to attend a dance—a journey that might have accounted for his whereabouts at the time of the Pandjiris assault—could not be corroborated by a single witness. Worse yet, witness Otto Hochstein recalled a murder-night conversation with Winters in which the latter had said, apropos of nothing in particular, "If anything happens, keep mum."

More damning still to Winters was the testimony bearing on his possible motive. Like Cecelia Gullivan, Winters worked at the Cone Automatic Machine Company. His fellow employees L. J. Boucher, Ralph Wood, Arthur E. Gibson, and Ernest C. Glace now took the stand to tell of vulgar sexual comments Winters had uttered about Gullivan as she walked through the tool room on various occasions, including his expressed desire, emphasized by crotch-grabbing gestures, to have sexual intercourse with her. (Winters had no way of knowing that, owing to a vaginal tumor, Cecelia Gullivan was probably incapable of sexual intercourse, forced or otherwise. This unanticipated impediment might have explained the ferocious brutality of her assailant.) G. W. Putnam, who had been with Winters early on the night of November 6, testified that Winters had been eager to find a woman with whom he could have a "good time."

All that remained to clinch the conviction of Winters was the appearance of Bessie Pandjiris, who testified on Friday afternoon, February 2. After she stated she had known Winters by sight since the early 1920s, she was asked to point him out in the courtroom. Raising her voice, she jabbed an accusing finger toward him and said, "Right there!" Attorney General Carver concluded the state's case by reading to the jury the text of statements Winters had made to the authorities shortly after his arrest—statements sharply inconsistent with testimony offered by prosecution witnesses.

Defense attorneys Tupper and Bicknell fought hard on behalf of Winters during the prolonged trial, which dragged on for almost a full month; but they failed to keep their client's damaging post-arrest statements out of the record, and they were unsuccessful in their repeated efforts to stop the prosecution from bundling the Pandjiris and Gullivan assaults together, particularly as to the motive of their perpetrator. Tupper and Bicknell argued that the motive in the assaults, especially the attack on Gullivan, might well have been robbery, not rape, and invoked the evidentiary rule that a fact susceptible of two interpretations should be granted the one more favorable to the defendant. But Judge Thompson rejected their argument, forcing them to rely upon the unconvincing denials contained in Winters's own trial testimony and ineffectual quibbling over Pandjiris's delayed identification of her attacker.

The case finally went to the jury at 10:35 on the morning of Friday, February 18, 1927. Just four hours later, the jury returned with a verdict of first-degree murder, the only penalty possible for which was death in the electric chair. Two weeks later Judge Thompson formally sentenced Winters to death, and his lawyers immediately filed an appeal to the Vermont Supreme Court.

Almost a year went by while Tupper and Bicknell awaited their opportunity to argue before the Vermont justices. No new evidence favorable to Winters developed during that time, and the outlook remained bleak as the final weeks before the January 1928 hearing sped by. And then, suddenly and out of the blue, came a ray of hope, the consummation of a desperate lawyer's dream: Clarence Darrow had agreed to take up the fight to save John Winters's life.

If you don't believe justice can be capricious, consider the improbable evolution of Darrow's intervention in the case. Twenty-four years before, back when Darrow was first winning his reputation as the last legal hope of the hopeless, Darrow's son Paul had been an undergraduate at Dartmouth College in Hanover, New Hampshire. And it was near Hanover on a June day in 1904 that Paul's runaway horse had fatally injured the five-year-old son of Mrs. Harry Cooley. It was a terrible, apparently unavoidable accident, but the Cooley family was so reasonable and understanding about the tragedy that a grateful Paul Darrow wrote a note to Mrs. Cooley, promising, on behalf of the Darrow clan, any future aid requested by the grieving mother. Mrs. Cooley was still alive in 1928, and with her nephew John Winters slated for execution, she wrote to Clarence Darrow and asked the eminent lawyer to redeem his son's long-ago pledge.

Nearly seventy-one years old and aged beyond his years by his fabled legal combats, Darrow, just the previous year, had finally made good on his frequent threats to retire. But a promise was a promise, so the 12th of January 1928 found him before the five Vermont Supreme Court justices, ready to battle for John Winters's life. As anticipated, Darrow's reputation brought an unprecedented crowd of curious spectators to the courtroom, a throng that spilled out into the corridors of the new court chambers. Like most Americans, Vermonters were well aware that this was the celebrated champion who had triumphed in some of the most seemingly hopeless legal contests of his era: the 1907 defense of "Big Bill" Haywood, accused of assassinating former Idaho governor Frank Steunenberg; his victory in the trial of the McNamara brothers, charged with the bombing of the *Los Angeles Times* building that killed twenty-one persons; his near-miraculous rescue of thrill-killers Leopold and Loeb from the electric chair in 1924; and his moral victory at the 1925 Scopes "Monkey Trial," where he demolished the reputation of William Jennings Bryan. Even the five justices were awed by his presence—although as attorney Paul Gillies has noted in his study of Darrow's Vermont episode, they generally behaved as if it were just another appeal hearing and Darrow just another lawyer. But their repeated references to Winters's "learned counsel" and their willingness to double the time normally allotted to the arguments of the opposing lawyers clearly signaled that the court recognized Darrow's celebrity status.

Readers familiar with Darrow's accustomed courtroom forensics are aware that he frequently ignored the facts of his cases, relying instead on emotional appeals to the jury's sense of fairness and sympathy for the underdog. But his argument in *State v. John C. Winters* adhered scrupulously to the original trial record and the relevant exceptions appealed by Bicknell and Tupper. These included

1. Dr. Kent's courtroom identification of the smudges on Gullivan's bed linen as footprints, an identification that the defense claimed was beyond his expertise;

2. The admission of testimony by Winters's fellow employees that he had made comments indicating his sexual interest in Gullivan, comments improperly used by the prosecution to emphasize that his motive in the Gullivan assault was rape, not robbery;

3. The admission of testimony concerning Winters's movements and behavior in the hours just before the assaults, especially his ambiguous request to Otto Hochstein to "keep mum";

4. Sheriff Fairbanks's dramatic reconstruction of the murder bedroom, a re-creation that could not possibly have replicated the room's exact state at the time of the murder;

5. The prosecution's skillful amalgamation of the Pandjiris and Gullivan assaults, particularly the contention that the motive of the first assault—rape—was identical to that of the second;

6. Bessie Pandjiris's failure to immediately identify her assailant, despite the fact that he was known to her;

7. The exclusion of potential testimony by Winters that might have offered an alternative explanation for how he had gotten blood on his trousers.

Darrow carefully addressed the elements of Tupper and Bicknell's exceptions, and with close attention to detail. He especially deplored the histrionics of Fairbanks's murder-scene replication and the prosecution's deliberate melding of the two assaults —assaults, he insisted, that were characterized by different motives. Excoriating the extremely graphic testimony about the attempted rape of Pandjiris, Darrow argued that "there can be no question what the effect of [such] evidence was if the jury was satisfied it was the same person in question. Its effect was to madden and craze the jury. . . . It had no place in a court of justice."

But Darrow reserved his highest rhetorical scorn for Judge Thompson's exclusion of Winters's testimony that he might have gotten the blood on his trousers when he accidentally sliced off part of a finger on an occasion prior to November 6, 1926. "Law," Darrow passionately insisted, "is not a system of tricks. It is a system of getting justice. I don't know what the jury would have done with the [blood] evidence. . . . But it had a right to it."

If the unexpected and dramatic appearance of America's greatest advocate was evidence of the capriciousness of justice, the sequel to the Winters appeal hearing furnished an even more dramatic illustration of such unpredictability. Although exactly what occurred during the deliberations of the Vermont Supreme Court justices over the Winters appeal is unknown, it was obvious to legal observers as the months passed without a decision that the five justices remained badly divided about the case, especially over the question of the suppressed testimony about Winters's bloody trousers. Then, in early 1929, John C. Winters got his second colossal break.

Ironically enough, it was President Calvin Coolidge—perhaps Clarence Darrow's most polar opposite—who ultimately, if unwittingly, helped save Winters's life. On January 19, 1929, with the Winters appeal still pending, Coolidge appointed his old friend, Vermont associate supreme court justice Harry B. Chase, to fill a judicial vacancy in the Circuit Court of the Second District. The Vermont legislature quickly elected Julius A. Willcox as his replacement, and in early March Darrow returned to Montpelier for a repeat performance so that the new justice could hear his argument concerning the evidence of the bloody trousers. A week later the court rendered its decision, setting aside Winters's first-degree murder conviction and ordering a new trial. Interestingly, the court upheld Judge Thompson's original trial rulings on every single exception, save that pertaining to the blood evidence. And the vote on that fiercely disputed element was a narrow 3–2, with the new justice, Willcox, casting the crucial swing vote that overturned Winters's conviction. Although Chief Justice John H. Watson dissented, he gamely wrote the majority decision—but, as Paul Gillies has commented, he "seemed to hold his nose" when writing about the blood evidence. Rather than directly confront his colleagues' legal reasoning, Watson chose to characterize the conflict over the exclusion of the blood evidence as the unintentional product of a supposed misunderstanding between Judge Thompson and Winters's defense counsel. Watson got some of his own back, however, in his prolix and sometimes caustic dismissal of all the other exceptions contained in the appeal.

Darrow did not show up later that year for Winters's second trial. Most probably he believed his family obligation had been fully honored. Moreover, he too may have had private reservations about his erstwhile client. Darrow, a severe social Darwinist, believed human beings were creatures always at the mercy of their genes and environment. He bluntly stated his credo to an audience of Norwich University cadets, just a few hours after his first appearance before the Vermont justices: "My experience has shown me that criminals, for the most part, are the poor, the weak and the uneducated. They have been without the opportunities and training that more fortunate people receive. . . . My sympathy is with them."

Given such views, Darrow probably did not believe that even the worst criminals were truly responsible for their acts, and he therefore opposed capital punishment without exceptions. He did, however, recognize that society needed to be protected from violent criminals, so he likely suffered few qualms when Winters was duly convicted of second-degree murder and sentenced to life in Windsor Prison. As is so often the case, it was not quite life. On August 24, 1949, after serving twenty years of his sentence, Winters was paroled by Governor Ernest Gibson. The main reason for his release seems to have been that he was suffering from tuberculosis, and the fifty-two-year-old Winters immediately departed Vermont to live out his sunset years in a home for the aged and infirm in New Mexico.

"ENTRANCED AND BESIDE HERSELF"

The 1897 Wheeler-Brewster Tragedy

> You are going far away,
> But remember what I say
> When you are in the city's giddy whirl,
> From temptations, crimes and follies,
> Villains, taxicabs and trolleys,
> Oh! Heaven will protect the working girl
>
> —"Heaven Will Protect the Working Girl," music by
> Charles K. Harris, lyrics by Edgar Smith (1909)

Adolescence isn't a crime. But to those caught in its gruesome agonies, it often seems like an undeserved punishment. And its torments are most painful for those in love, be they Shakespeare's Romeo and Juliet or the obscurest wallflowers of the latest freshman class. Is there anyone so ancient that he or she cannot recall an unrequited affection that drove them to despair or even desperate action? Or a moment when the rejection of their love seemed like the end of the world? Most of us survive the perils of such youthful infatuations, although we may carry their emotional scars and mortifying memories to the grave. But some of us don't—and such is the terrible tale of Mildred Brewster and Anna Wheeler. They may have lived in the bygone Vermont of 1897, a time of endless toil, horse-drawn transport, kerosene lamps, and handmade shirtwaists. But their story remains as fresh as yesterday's broken heart and as shocking as, well, a bullet to the head.

Even the least superstitious folk might allow that the omens conspired against Mildred Brewster even before she drew her first breath. Born to a clan of prosperous farmers in Huntington Center in 1876 and christened Lena Merrilla, she would eventually insist that everyone call her Mildred. Even those who would not later excuse her moral defects would admit she was reared in a family renowned for eccentricity, willful temperament, and a penchant for suicide. Her maternal grandfather, Arnold Sherman, culminated a career of threats of self-destruction by fatally cutting his throat. Several of Mildred's aunts on both sides were reputed to be of unsound mind: Her maternal aunt killed herself with poison, and Arnold Sherman's sister, Eunice Chaffee, periodically scandalized her relatives and amused her neighbors by transferring her living quarters to the family pigsty. Indeed, at Mildred's 1898 murder trial, evidence of mental instability reaching back five generations would be solicited to prove her the inevitable fruit of a degenerate family tree. But there's no doubt the gravest blow to Mildred's life prospects came three years before she was even born. In July of 1873 her future mother, Emma, lost her only daughter, Minnie, in a household scalding accident, causing her to lapse into a slough of depression and ill-health that would endure the rest of her life. As her kith and kin would later testify, Emma showed little interest in her second daughter and last child, and their relations alternated between apathy and antipathy from the moment of Mildred's birth.

Mildred's mental heritage was admittedly inauspicious; her physiological inheritance may have been a greater handicap. From the age of three she suffered terribly from frequent headaches and "spasms," during which she would sometimes lose consciousness and suffer memory loss. Even those well disposed to her thought her difficult, stubborn, and disquietingly unpredictable as she grew into her teenage years in Huntington Center. Chronically moody, she apparently attempted suicide with a bottle of laudanum when she was fifteen. Her disposition not improving after her mother died in 1892, her father, Wesley Brewster, permitted her to live in

Burlington, where she attended high school while boarding and waitressing at E. H. Shattuck's restaurant. Both Mr. and Mrs. Shattuck and several of their other boarders would later testify that Mildred seemed of unsound mind during her two-year sojourn with them. Subject to unpredictable and frequent mood swings, she would sometimes go for days or even weeks without speaking to anyone. Indeed, a number of her Burlington acquaintances remarked that she sometimes didn't appear to recognize familiar acquaintances or even close relatives. At other times she would lock herself in her bedroom for days, repelling all social contact and refusing to eat. Owing, perhaps, to such personal impediments, Mildred failed to graduate on time from Burlington High School, but she eventually managed to earn her diploma and a temporary teaching certificate.

Mildred's 1895 return to the family farm didn't last long. She failed to get along with her two brothers and their wives, and after ten weeks of teaching at the Huntington elementary school, she threw in the towel. Against her father's wishes and his willingness to support her indefinitely, she insisted she must go and make her own way and her own living in the big city. That fall, she took the stage to Montpelier and soon settled in there as a live-in domestic servant in the home of S. C. Shurtleff.

Unsurprisingly, Mildred didn't last long at the Shurtleff residence. Being a person of habitual moodiness and antagonism who was accustomed to being indulged, Mildred did not suffer in silence Mrs. Shurtleff's reproofs for her misbehavior—mostly staying out late in the evenings. Skillful with a needle when she chose to be, Mildred soon found work in D. D. Haley's tailoring shop. Eventually she moved on to the larger workshop of Ledden & Campbell and began looking for a less socially restrictive place to live.

Wesley Brewster had worried much about the fate of his mercurial daughter in the big city—and he had both good reason and ample company. Millions of other American fathers and mothers fretted during the 1890s as their daughters fled the stifling society and unremunerative toil of family farms for better prospects. Parents feared what might happen to such young, inexperienced females when they encountered the gaudy temptations, moral laxity, and absence of familial control found in even such a modest metropolis as Montpelier. Many such young women did succumb to the pitfalls of urban life, and often suffered the fate worse than death—the moral obloquy and social death of "getting in trouble." As events would prove, Mildred, a 125-pound brunette and reasonably attractive young woman, was one of them—but literally one with a vengeance.

Mildred's fatal encounter with destiny took place on Easter Sunday, April 5, 1897. While visiting friends at the Montpelier boardinghouse of John Goodenough, she met John Wheeler, a handsome, twenty-year-old stonecutter employed in the Fraser & Broadfoot granite sheds. Just commencing the critical period of her much-delayed social adolescence, Mildred had little experience of men, and she fell hard for "Jack" Wheeler. Personable, popular, a member of the Montpelier Young Men's Christian Association chapter, and a strutting corporal in the Vermont National Guard, Jack was no stranger to courting girls, and he and Mildred were soon spending several nights a week together, most of them passed, like those of other Montpelier couples, in promenading the streets and intimate conversation. Shortly after meeting Wheeler, Mildred went off to Northfield, where she worked in a hotel for several weeks. Continuing his attentions, Jack corresponded with Mildred and, accompanied by others, visited her several times. When she returned to Montpelier in late May, Mildred became Wheeler's fellow boarder at the Goodenough residence.

Sometime during that spring, she also became his bedmate. Mildred would later insist that it was only after Jack promised to marry her that she surrendered her virtue. That may or may not have been true: If Jack Wheeler made such a promise, he was never foolish enough to do so in front of witnesses. But Jack's core feelings about Mildred were best expressed by a later, unsentimental admission wrung from him in court: "She was willing and so was I." In any case, their nocturnal visits to each other's rooms continued with increasing brazenness and frenzy through the summer of 1896. It probably came as a surprise only to Mildred when she realized in August she was pregnant.

Mildred would later claim that it was Jack who insisted she abort their child. But whatever her compunctions about that taboo act, she wasn't about to return to her family in shame with a bastard child. The upshot was that sometime that September, she swallowed an unidentified abortifacient and pushed some metal implement into her womb to destroy her child. It worked, but it must have been a horrific ordeal. It seems likely that she performed the painful act one autumn day just before John Goodenough and his wife arrived home to find her pale, fatigued, and depressed. The Goodenoughs also noticed a "foul odor" in her room, a telltale smell that the worldly John Goodenough later admitted he hardly dared believe. But nothing was said, although Mildred continued her personal deterioration, sinking further into despondency and eating practically nothing, during her last two months at the Goodenough boardinghouse.

Even without her prejudicial heritage, Mildred had good reason to be depressed. Much to her consternation and apparent surprise, Jack Wheeler's attentions lessened progressively in the weeks after her pregnancy was aborted. Worse yet, she began to hear disquieting rumors that he had found another sweetheart. True, he had always enjoyed a reputation as a ladies' man, but the word on the Montpelier street and among the seamstresses at Ledden & Campbell's shop that autumn was that his new love was serious. Her name was Anna Wheeler (no relation to Jack, despite the identical surname), she was pretty, just seventeen years old, and she had recently come from her parents' East Montpelier farm to work as a domestic servant in the East Liberty Street home of her cousin, Mrs. C. E. Bugbee. All in all, she was everything that Mildred Brewster had been when she first met Jack Wheeler: young, innocent, and in grateful awe of the attentions paid her by the handsome granite worker.

Mildred didn't take her rejection well. Socially maladjusted and emotionally far younger than her twenty years, she nourished her jealousy in brooding anger and vindictive fantasy as the months rolled by. In December of 1896 she put some distance between herself and the increasingly remote Jack by moving out of the Goodenough house and into a room at Patrick McBride's house on Barre Street. But her anger mounted daily, and as 1896 expired and rumors spread that Jack and Anna were formally engaged, Mildred began dropping frequent if vague threats against Jack and Anna into her conversations with fellow workers and boarders. When Jack's best friend, Joseph Rogers, mentioned Jack's engagement to Anna, Mildred scoffed at the notion but warned that Jack would never have Anna for his wife. And she told her friend Mary O'Neil that Jack had reneged on a promise to marry her and that his rumored marriage to Anna would never take place.

Mildred's descent into unreasoning fury escalated sharply during the last two weeks of May 1897. Sometime that spring she had a conversation with Emma Carey, her fellow worker at the Ledden

& Campbell shop, in which she inquired as to the best way to commit suicide. Increasingly careless at her work, she was fired from her job in mid-May. It was probably also during this period that she composed several documents expressing her intense feelings about the man who had rejected her and the woman who had supplanted her. The first two were poison-pen letters, one addressed to Anna Wheeler. Posing as her anonymous "East Montpelier Friend," Mildred denounced Jack Wheeler as a heartless seducer. Stating that she had incontestable proof that he had gotten a girl "in trouble," she warned, "The people say he isn't much any way and they are forming a poor opinion of you down here. . . . Now Anna I know that you are a nice girl and I think you had better ship him and by the way avoid public scandal. I always thought he had too smooth a tongue."

Perhaps fearing that Anna was too smitten to credit her accusations, Mildred sent another poison-pen letter, this one to Temperance Wheeler, Anna's mother. In it she repeated her claim that Jack had impregnated an unidentified female and appealed to a mother's concern for her daughter's imperiled reputation: "To shield your daughter from dishonor I write you this. If your daughter is a nice young lady as I believe her to be she will not hesitate to send him word at once that she does not care for his company any longer." Unable to conceal her personal spite, Anna added, "P. S. This girl can have him in trouble any time she likes. I do hope she will, it would serve him right."

Apparently both of Mildred's missives were ignored, as Anna continued to keep company with her acknowledged fiancé. Around the same time Mildred wrote an unaddressed letter, which was never sent. In fact it may not have been intended for anyone in particular, but in it Mildred poured all the toxic feelings that had been festering in her stunted and aching soul throughout her young life:

Don't blame love-sick girls for they were made thus loving. A handsome girl is something to one, real good, willing, self-sacrificing man. But one who loves almost to distraction is the best. Take those lukewarm, indifferent, lifeless beauties, you would become marital martyrs; but she is the premium wife, whose fervid, glowing, devoted, whole-souled love knows no limit, who is spellbound, magnetized, entranced and beside herself when beside her lover, whose love, torrent like, sweeps all before it, making all possible allowance for imperfections in the loved one, and magnifying to the highest degree all his desirable and lovable traits of character.

Having thus stated, if only to herself, her uncompromising emotional credo, Mildred methodically prepared herself for the final act of her planned personal melodrama. As the last days of May slipped by, she began seasoning her threats against Jack and Anna with cryptic warnings to her friends that something would soon happen that would "shock them." Virtually all who saw Mildred during the last week of May would later testify that her alarming appearance during that period went beyond her usual eccentricity and disorder. There was a wild look in her eyes, she sometimes acted as though she feared someone was following her, and she often vacillated without warning or apparent cause between moods of hilarity and despondency. After her employment was terminated, she told several persons she intended to go back home to Huntington on May 31. Her last letter to her father was replete with the unhappiness that had gradually swallowed up her life: "Everything has gone wrong with me ever since I came here, but it will all be over some day when the robins play La Crosse [over her grave]. . . . I am your rough and tumble little girl alone and uncared for by many. Ha, ha."

Whatever she told others, Mildred had no intention of returning home. She would only know a different, if equally familiar, unhappiness there—and she had resolved to put a decisive end to her current difficulties. Early on the afternoon of Friday, May 28, she walked into the G. J. Reynolds store in the Granite Block in Barre. She asked for clerk John Wallace and told him she wished to buy a revolver to take back to her brother in Huntington the following week. After testing a half-dozen weapons, she selected a .32 caliber Iver Johnson five-chambered, double-acting center-fire model. She told Wallace she chose it because it was both the prettiest and easiest weapon to use. She also purchased a box of fifty cartridges.

Mildred's next stop was the Barre home of her childhood friend, Alice Ross. Although Ross was used to her friend's quicksilver disposition, Mildred seemed more agitated than ever that afternoon. After telling the married Ross how much she yearned to be wed, Mildred insisted that they visit a fortune-teller on Granite Street. After consulting the seer, Mildred told the skeptical Alice that the clairvoyant had told her that she had "always been in trouble and more trouble was in store for her." Mildred claimed she scorned such superficial soothsaying, telling the seer, "You need not have told me that, as I have always been in trouble and always expect to be."

Mildred's odd behavior continued through that evening. At her boardinghouse she conversed for some time with fellow boarders Helen Clay and Mr. and Mrs. Alex Glinney. After borrowing some paper from Mr. Glinney to pack flowers with, she sat down at the parlor organ and played "Put Away the Little Dresses That Our Darling Used to Wear." Mildred then asked Helen to play the hymn "Jesus, Lover of My Soul." Helen complied but stopped after Mildred abruptly ceased singing when she got to the end of the verse, "When the storm of life is passed." Before she left the group, Mildred displayed and offered three of her new revolver cartridges to Alex and asked his wife to go target shooting with her sometime.

As she left the house, she told Mrs. Glinney she would spend the next day with her.

Mildred was next seen by Montpelier resident Alex Waycott on a Montpelier street. Mildred was acquainted with Waycott, and she asked him if it was all right if she used a tree there for target practice with her revolver. Waycott, who had always thought her a peculiar girl, told her she had better take her target practice outside the city limits. Later that night, Mildred was seen lurking around the Montpelier National Guard Armory. Jack Wheeler, a member of Company H, was drilling with his unit there that evening. It was later surmised but not proven that Mildred intended to assassinate him as he left the armory. As it happened, his friends accompanied him home, and Mildred probably relinquished her plan to shoot him on the street as impractical.

Sometime that night or early the next morning Mildred altered the focus of her rage. After arising at 5 AM, she walked to the Clay Hill area at the eastern limits of Montpelier, near the old town mill and the Montpelier Seminary campus. She was spotted during her walk there by Mildred Waycott and three other eyewitnesses, Harmon and Alfred Deslaurias and John Lawrence, who saw and heard her practicing with her revolver on the hill. A little before 7 AM, at last satisfied with her prowess, Mildred headed for fifty-four East Liberty Street, the C. E. Bugbee residence and current home of Anna Wheeler.

Anna was already up, and the two women conversed together for more than an hour. Little of what they said is known, but Mrs. Bugbee overheard enough to discern that Mildred and Anna were contesting which of them was actually Jack Wheeler's fiancée. Shortly before 8 AM, Mrs. Bugbee heard Mildred exclaim, "We can't both of us be engaged to Jack Wheeler; we must meet him face to face!" A minute later, Anna and Mildred were out the door and on their way to Sibley Avenue, where Jack was living with his aged mother, Mary, and brother Sam in a cottage.

Mildred and Anna never got there. A century ago the Montpelier Seminary area, now occupied by the Vermont College campus, was a more rugged and challenging terrain than at present for those traveling north or south. Sibley Avenue made a wide bend as it branched out from College Street, but one could take a shortcut through a sort of ravine fringed by sandy banks and rocky ledges. Domestic servants Gertrude and Helen Donahue, toiling in the home of Professor D. S. Blanpied on College Street, saw the two women walking under Mildred's umbrella in the light rain as they descended out of sight into the ravine. Pedestrian George Manning was probably the last person to see Anna Wheeler alive. When he passed her and Mildred near the top of the path, he noticed that Mildred, clad in a black skirt, was talking and looking very serious but that Anna was smiling.

A few seconds later, at about 8:15 AM, two shots rang out in quick succession. Startled by the noise of the first shot, Gertrude Donahue looked out the window and saw one of the girls fall to the ground. A second later another shot rang out, and Gertrude ran out of the house toward the shooting scene. She was joined by Sam Wheeler, who had heard the shots from his brother's house. Gertrude and Sam found Mildred and Anna lying on the ravine path, one slightly to the right, the other to the left. They were both near death, and pools of their blood and brains almost mingled together where they lay. Minutes later, Montpelier policeman C. E. Demerritt arrived, as did physician Charles E. Chandler. At Dr. Chandler's instruction, the wounded women were first carried to the porch of Jack Wheeler's house and then conveyed to Montpelier's Heaton Hospital. No one doubted from the second the bodies were discovered that Mildred Brewster had first shot Anna Wheeler at point-blank range, just below the right ear, and then shot herself in the same place.

Dr. Chandler immediately diagnosed Anna's head wound as fatal, but he labored strenuously for the next six hours to save her life. But when he went probing for the bullet he discovered it had traversed her brain, and she never regained consciousness before dying at 2:30 that Saturday afternoon. Mildred regained consciousness several hours later and was able to converse with her father, Wesley, in the hospital. She told him she remembered nothing about the shootings and that she had only meant to kill herself. When told she had shot Anna Wheeler, she said she hoped Anna would survive and begged Wesley repeatedly to procure some morphine so she could commit suicide. The horrified Wesley would later confess that he wished for her sake she had died of her wound immediately.

Meanwhile, Montpelier sheriff Charles Bancroft began to sift through the evidence to determine the how and why of Mildred's terrible deeds. He was anticipated, however, by Jack Wheeler's friend Joseph Rogers. Shortly after the shootings, Rogers had entered Mildred's room and found six letters in a bureau drawer. One was a twenty-six-page epistle to Jack Wheeler. He brought it to Wheeler and began reading it to him, but when Jack started crying they decided to burn it then and there. Another letter was to her landlord, Patrick McBride, in which Mildred defended her reputation, acknowledged her crime, and addressed the practical consequences of her intended death:

> Mr. McBride: The report you have heard about Joe Rogers and myself is probably the reason you want my room. That report is not true, but the next report you hear will be true. No fellow

can be engaged to me and run around with other girls all that he likes, and if I have got to die, others will have to die too. My clothes are all clean and all you will have to do is to put on my waist, which hangs in my room.

Without notifying the authorities, Rogers took the five extant letters home and concealed them for five months beneath some floorboards before turning them over to Mildred's defense attorneys.

Once it became clear Mildred would survive, the only question was whether she could avoid hanging by convincing a jury she was not guilty by reason of insanity. Dr. Chandler finally managed to remove the bullet from her brain during an operation—without anesthetic—in January 1898, and her only noticeable physical souvenir of her wound was an involuntary drawing together of the facial muscles, producing an unsightly contraction of her mouth.

Mildred's attorneys, William A. Lord, Frederick P. Carleton, and Frank Plumley, immediately began securing witnesses to attest to Mildred's mental instability, ultimately recruiting nearly half a hundred. They also gained additional time to prepare their case with a shrewd legal maneuver. When Mildred's trial commenced on November 22, 1897, Lord immediately demanded that her murder indictment be quashed on the ground that a stenographer had been present during the grand jury's hearing of testimony. Lord's challenge automatically triggered an appeal to the Vermont Supreme Court, and so another five months elapsed before Lord's objection was overruled by that tribunal and Mildred's trial was allowed to begin on April 4, 1898, a full ten months after the shootings.

Everyone concerned knew it would be a lengthy trial, but no one expected the monthlong marathon that ensued. With Judge Loveland Munson presiding, assisted by side judges Mark Mears and Charles E. Jones, Mildred's counsel was opposed by veteran prosecutors Judge Zed Stanton and state's attorney Fred Howland. With nearly 150 witnesses testifying, the trial set a new record with the sheer physical bulk of the pages it took to document its proceedings. Most of the trial sessions were packed with eager spectators, some of them sneeringly termed "Kodak fiends" because of the newfangled cameras they brought with them to photograph the trial's principals. Some observers, too, noted with disapproval how many ladies attended the trial, which promised to include many disclosures of a salacious and sensational nature.

The tedious process of jury selection consumed the first two days. As soon as it was completed, however, attorney Lord tried another clever legal ploy, demanding the jury members be discharged on the ground that none of them had been asked if the fact that Mildred was a female would influence their verdict in a capital case. Judge Munson quickly overruled the motion, and the trial finally began in earnest on the afternoon of April 6.

Stanton and Howland's case against Mildred was a classic murder prosecution, without histrionics or gimmicks. Focusing on motive, means, and opportunity, the prosecutors used their witnesses to build a painstaking, seamless, and detailed narrative of how Mildred's virulent jealousy of Anna Wheeler had led her to purchase a revolver and cold-bloodedly put a bullet in Anna's head. The only relatively expert testimony presented by the state was given by William J. Kinsley, a New Jersey handwriting expert, who identified some of Mildred's letters, including her poison-pen missives, as being in her handwriting. On the fourth day of the trial, the jury toured the murder scene. Mildred's lawyers never disputed the basic facts of the shooting during the six days of direct testimony before the state rested its case on Tuesday, April 12.

The real struggle now began, as the defense lawyers maneuvered to create sympathy for Mildred. One of their chief, if unwilling, assets proved to be Jack Wheeler. Jack, it developed, had already unwittingly done much to aid the cause of the defense. Just a few hours after Anna's murder, with her blood and brains still fresh on the path near College Street, he had submitted to a most imprudent interview with Edwin A. Nutt, a veteran reporter for the *Vermont Watchman & State Journal*. During that interview he had emphatically denied ever having "kept company" or having had more than a casual acquaintance with Mildred, and he insisted vehemently and repeatedly that he had never solicited or reciprocated her affections. But, following Nutt's persuasive testimony about Jack's post-murder denials, Lord demolished Wheeler on the stand, forcing him to retract his self-serving lies about his relations with Mildred and to admit the sordid, sad facts of her seduction, pregnancy, abortion, and abandonment. As a reporter for the *Burlington Free Press* dryly put it, Wheeler's admissions placed him "in a light that is far from enviable." Mildred, who had hitherto spent the trial sessions rocking impassively in a comfortable rocking chair provided her, completed Jack's demonization by breaking down and sobbing uncontrollably during his testimony.

It only remained for the defense to document Mildred's mental instability, a task to which they brought nearly forty witnesses, many of them testifying that Mildred and quite a number of her relatives, going back generations, had been mentally infirm, dangerously eccentric, or outright deranged. Several dozen witnesses, who had known Mildred during her childhood, her Burlington years, or her twenty months in Montpelier, testified to her unpredictable mood swings and frequently bizarre and inappropriate behavior. Fred Highley, Mildred's cousin, told of how she laughed and ran bareheaded through the Huntington Center village streets on the day of her mother's 1892 funeral. Many of the defense witnesses recalled occasions when Mildred would greet them effusively, only to subsequently shock them by seeming not to recognize them. Ellen Moody of South Starksboro told the jury she had witnessed Mildred suffering severe physical fits at the ages of three and nine, and that Mildred's mother had told her that Mildred had had similar fits while still in the womb. More dramatically, Mary O'Neil, Mildred's friend and co-worker at the Ledden & Campbell shop, remembered an occasion when Mildred had unsuccessfully attempted to jump out of an upper-story window.

Mildred's counsel devoted much effort to proving her the helpless victim of inherited mental instability. Several witnesses, including Brewster family physician Dr. F. D. Falley, told of her mother's chronic depression and mental deterioration after the scalding death of her first daughter. More of Mildred's relatives and acquaintances chronicled the mental instability and eventual suicides of her paternal grandfather and great-uncle. And nearly a dozen witnesses took the stand to retail the entertaining eccentricities of Mildred's great-aunt, who had occasionally moved her living quarters into the family pigpen and had conversations with her dead husband. By the time the defense had completed its case, the family's mental frailties had been traced back to a Captain Farr, who had commanded a company of American soldiers during the War of 1812 and afterward died "a raving maniac."

Attacking the insanity defense head-on, the state called thirty-nine witnesses in rebuttal. Predictably, every one of them testified that while Mildred and her relatives were notoriously eccentric and willful, none of them was truly insane. A detailed recitation of their counter-testimony would be tedious in the extreme, but a *Randolph News & Herald* reporter aptly summarized their reflections on Mildred's mental condition with the remark, "Most of them said she had a bad disposition, was ugly and queer, but not insane."

Neither the prosecution nor the defense was much aided by

their presentations of expert witnesses. Dr. Frank W. Page, the superintendent of the State Hospital for the Insane, and Dr. Charles W. Page of the Danvers, Massachusetts, insane asylum opined that Mildred was insane at the time of the shootings. The state countered with Dr. S. E. Lawton from the Brattleboro asylum and Boston insanity expert Dr. T. W. Fisher, who argued that Mildred was sane and knew the difference between right and wrong when she decided to shoot Anna Wheeler. Probably the most telling index of the learned doctors' confusing and jargon-laden testimony came on Friday afternoon, April 29, when two jurors were observed to be fast asleep during Dr. Lawton's testimony. It seems probable, given the trial's outcome, that the most perceptive and influential medical insight came from Dr. Page, who characterized Mildred's murder-day state as simply "the insanity of a seduced woman."

The last of the rebuttal witnesses testified on Saturday, April 30, and final arguments began two days later, with Frank Plumley pinch-hitting for William Lord, who was too ill to appear. Judge Munson's charge to the jury was a model of fairness, emphasizing the difficulty of determining Mildred's mental state at the time of her terrible act, given such copious but contradictory testimony. In the end, Munson was probably as baffled as the jurors by the numbing and arcane jargon of Drs. Page, Lawton, Fisher, and Page, telling the jury, "To a considerable extent, both the state and the defense rely upon the same evidence in support of their different theories. In some instances the same thing is urged by one side as proof of sane calculations and by the other as proof of a disordered mind. Bring these conflicting claims to the test of your own judgment and say which is right."

The case finally went to the jury at 2:30 PM on Wednesday, May 4, almost exactly a month after it began. Eighteen hours later the twelve men returned with a verdict of "not guilty by reason of insanity"—and the case was suddenly over after thirty-two days. Little is known of the deliberations, except the remark by one of the jurors that there had never been a chance that Mildred would be found guilty of first-degree murder. The following Monday Judge Munson ordered Mildred to be incarcerated at the Vermont State Hospital for the Insane in Waterbury, pending his court's further direction. The next morning Mildred left on the train to begin her new life there.

It may be presumed that that life was not a happy one. Mildred had repeatedly stated during her trial that while she preferred not to be hanged, she had no desire to live in normal society again. Perhaps she was sincere, but she certainly changed her mind as the years went by. Her father died in 1901, personally and financially ruined by the effects of his daughter's crime. In 1908 Mildred's insistent petitions to be released finally gained her a sanity hearing on April 21 before Judge Alfred A. Hall in Montpelier. The testimony Judge Hall heard that day and the next was rather mixed. Dr. F. E. Steele Sr. and Dr. R. N. Pelton, both supervisors at the Waterbury hospital, stated they considered Mildred sane and no threat to society. Indeed, they went so far as to say that she had probably not been insane when admitted to the hospital in 1898. But hospital superintendent Dr. Don D. Grout and staff physician Dr. Watson Wasson vehemently disagreed. Presumably enjoying more hands-on experience with Mildred, they bluntly characterized her as a "degenerate" and a continuing menace to society. After listening to the opinions of the physicians and talking to Mildred herself, Judge Hall ordered her immediate release to the custody of her childhood friend, Alice Ross. Noting that Mildred was still "eccentric and at times erratic," he nonetheless conceded that she did not seem a danger to the community and should go free. Judge Hall warned Mildred, however, that if her condition changed in that regard, his court would be "the first to see that measures were taken for your restraint." As she had since the shootings, Mildred insisted to Judge Hall that she had no memory of her awful deed and that she held no malice against anyone involved.

Alas, it would seem that Mildred's "condition" did change for the worse, and rather quickly at that. She comported herself well during her first weeks at the Ross home in Hardwick. But as the summer waned, she reverted to her basic personality, becoming increasingly stubborn, willful, and disobedient. The final straw for the Rosses came when she grew infatuated with a young laboring man of the town. The Rosses managed to warn him away from her—but that didn't stop the besotted Mildred, who continued her now unwelcome visits to his home and began following him around. By September the Rosses had endured enough, and they petitioned Judge Hall to take her back. And so, on the afternoon of September 22, 1908, she was surprised by a sheriff's posse in the Ross home and whisked away to the Montpelier jail. The next morning she returned to Waterbury, where tradition has it she lived out her days, forlorn and forgotten, until her death sometime in the 1940s. This chronicler has been unable to document her life further than the 1910 U.S. federal census. Presumably she whiled away her ample hours in the asylum with fancy needlework, the skill she had honed in the days when she was a high-strung young woman in Montpelier and dreamed of life with her handsome stonecutter.

Eighty years after the shootings, the Brewster tragedy had one last, worthy echo with the publication of acclaimed writer Susan Fromberg Schaeffer's novel *The Madness of a Seduced Woman*. Based on the Brewster case, it adhered when possible to the known facts of the story, including gritty details of such episodes as Mildred's abortion, the scalding death of Minnie Brewster, and great-aunt Eunice's predilection for pigsty domesticity. Given Jack

Wheeler's sullen prevarications and Mildred's stoic silence, much remains unknown about their liaison, and Schaeffer took advantage of that lacuna to conjure up the personalities of the two lovers and their fateful collision. More important from an artistic stance, Schaeffer was brilliantly, indeed, disquietingly successful at imagining and conveying the destructive passion that lay at the heart of Mildred Brewster's "fervid, glowing, devoted, whole-souled love."

CHAPTER 10

THE LOST CHILD

The 1946 Vanishing of Paula Welden

> Grief fills the room up of my absent child,
> Lies in his bed, walks up and down with me,
> Puts on his pretty looks, repeats his words,
> Remembers me of all his gracious parts,
> Stuffs out his vacant garments with his form.
>
> —Shakespeare, *King John*, Act III, Scene 4

I s there anything worse than the death of a child? Yes. Although it would seem to be a rhetorical question, there *is* something more tragic and heartbreaking than the untimely demise of the young. For even if a child is murdered, its mother and father usually have the comfort of finality, of knowing the worst and experiencing the full reality of their child's extinction. But for the parents of the permanently missing, there is no such solace, no such closure. Days, years, and even decades may pass without their ever knowing what happened to their beloved offspring or even whether the child is alive or dead. For the parents of the missing, their child's unknown fate persists as a lifelong, never-healing wound.

Like larger states, Vermont has its share of missing persons. In 2004 the Vermont Crime Information Center received 1,039 reports of missing persons, many of them children and adolescents—a volume that persists, as a visit to the Vermont Department of Public Safety Web site (http://www.dps.state.vt.us/vtsp/missing/) will confirm. And as crime connoisseurs well know, Vermont was a pioneer in the lore of American missing persons.

Probably the most fascinating case ever to occur in the United States was Manchester's Boorn mystery in the early 1800s. The 1812 disappearance of farmer Russell Colvin under suspicious circumstances ultimately put his brother-in-law Stephen Boorn on Vermont's death row. Boorn was ultimately exonerated when Russell belatedly reappeared, scant days before Stephen's scheduled execution. During the century that followed, the Boorn case was exploited as a cautionary tale in the campaign against capital punishment and even inspired one of Wilkie Collins's better shocker novels, *The Dead Alive*. (For a more cynical view of what happened in the Boorn affair, see Gerald McFarland's fascinating investigation, *The Counterfeit Man: The True Story of the Boorn-Colvin Murder Case*).

Notwithstanding the antique appeal of the Boorn mystery, the vintage years for Vermont missing persons seem to have been the post–World War II era, featuring such highlights as the Phalen, Tetford, and Carlo cases. Frank J. Phalen was a sixty-two-year-old engineer from Rutland. Awakening early on the morning of November 13, 1952, he told his wife, "I'm going to take a walk." He was never seen again. James E. Tetford, sixty-nine years old, was a World War I veteran and resident of the Soldiers' Home in Bennington. While returning home on a bus from St. Albans on December 1, 1949, he inexplicably vanished from his seat forever. So, too, did John Carlo, a thirty-six-year-old, long-term resident of the Brandon Training School with a mental age of three, who disappeared on September 2, 1954, never to be seen again. But there is little doubt that the most fascinating and unsolved missing-person case of that or any Vermont era remains the still-baffling disappearance of Paula Jean Welden on December 1, 1946.

Actually, Vermont's most famous missing person was not a native of the Green Mountain State. The eldest of the four daughters of W. Archibald Welden, a well-to-do industrial designer for the Revere Copper & Brass Company, Paula came from her Stamford, Connecticut, home to Vermont in 1945 to enroll at Bennington College. The fall of 1946 found the eighteen-year-old Paula a well-liked, academically successful, and apparently well-adjusted member of the sophomore class. She hoped to major in art, where her interests lay in drawing, oil painting, and sketching in charcoal and pencil. Physically active, she enjoyed hiking, swimming, square dancing, camping, and playing her guitar. Although an eye-catching, blue-eyed blonde, the five-foot, five-inch, 126-pound sophomore was considered somewhat on the shy side, reasonably social but with no known attraction to or relationship with a member of the opposite sex.

December 1, 1946, Paula's fateful day, began innocently enough. Although she had stayed up to party with some classmates the night before, she showed up and performed her usual duties working at the Bennington student cafeteria for the breakfast and lunch shifts. She then returned for several hours to the Dewey Hall dormitory room she shared with eighteen-year-old roommate Elizabeth Johnson. At least that was Johnson's best memory of the interval; Johnson's ability to "zone out" while studying was notorious among her friends.

About 2:30 that Sunday afternoon, Paula announced to Elizabeth that she wanted to take a hike before resuming her studies. Elizabeth thought nothing of her announcement; she knew Paula was an experienced, enthusiastic hiker, and the two of them had recently endured a rain-soaked night out camping in the Manchester area. Nor did she make anything of the fact that Paula didn't ask that she accompany her on her walk or tell her exactly where she was going. Minutes later, Paula left Dewey Hall forever. Although it was chilly, with a possibility of snow forecast for the higher elevations, Paula was lightly dressed for her expedition. Clad in a red parka with a fur-trimmed hood, she was wearing blue jeans and heavy-soled Top-Sider sneakers, size six and a half or seven. As far as could be later determined, she was carrying little if any cash, and she left behind in her room an uncashed check sent by her parents for her personal monthly expenses. She was probably wearing her elegant Elgin ladies' watch.

A few minutes after leaving Dewey Hall, Paula was spotted by two of her college friends in their car. They saw her as she walked toward the college gate at Highway 67A and then pulled abreast of her, offering her a ride into Bennington. She declined and continued on her way. As she emerged from the college gate by the highway, she was seen by Danny Fager, who was working at a nearby gas station. He watched with curiosity as she abruptly turned and walked up a small hill and into the woods, turned around and came back to the highway, and continued walking.

Like many a college student of the era, Paula thought nothing about the possible dangers of hitchhiking. Nor did most motorists of the day. It was only about 2:45 PM when contractor Louis Knapp saw the girl with her thumb out and stopped his pickup truck to give her a lift. He would later recall that she stumbled on the running board as she got in his vehicle. After cautioning her to watch her step, he asked her where she wanted to go. She told him she needed to get to Route 9, as she wished to walk on the Long Trail. (The Long Trail is a rugged Vermont hiking path whose construction predated the better-known Appalachian Trail. In 1946, as now, the two trails coincided in southern Vermont and intersected with Vermont State Route 9 about 12 miles east of Bennington.) She was in luck, Knapp replied, as his destination was his home on Route 9, just three miles from the Long Trail. Some time later, Knapp dropped her off by his house and she continued on her way. Knapp would later identify photographs of Paula as strongly resembling the female hitchhiker in his pickup truck that afternoon.

It would seem that Paula Welden made her way successfully to the Long Trail, for there were quite a number of witnesses who later stated that they had seen a striking-looking blonde of her description pass that way. Two of them were teenagers Robert and Edward Welch, who spotted her from their mother's house near the Long Trail entrance. "There goes a good-looking girl!" said one of them, and the other brother sprinted out of the house to get a better look. At first he thought it was a neighbor, but finally concluded that it wasn't as she disappeared from sight. Other residents, too, including Stearns Rice, Miss Mary F. Rice, and Lyman Royce, saw a girl matching Paula's description as she entered the Long Trail and began walking north toward Glastenbury Mountain. Forty-four years later, in an interview with *Bennington Banner* reporter Mary Baillie, area resident Walter Mould recalled seeing Paula as she walked into oblivion:

> [My wife and I] were one of the last ones to see Paula Welden go up the road the night she disappeared. It was gloomy—just starting to snow. And this girl was coming up the road, heading up the mountain all alone, thumbing a ride. We thought it was very strange. I'm positive it was her. . . . Everything fit. It was the time she went into [Bickford] hollow, she was all alone, her clothes—there's no question about it.

It was a little after 4 PM when the last known, or at least the last likely, sighting of Paula occurred. It was near the Fay Fuller shelter, where Ernie Whitman, a night watchman at the offices of the *Bennington Banner* newspaper, was gathered with three of his friends. They were starting out to return from their camp in Bickford Hollow to Bennington when suddenly a young woman approached Whitman, who was a bit ahead of his three companions, and asked him how far the Long Trail extended. He told her he had traveled only a few miles of it but that it went as far north as Canada. She thanked him politely and continued on her way, watched by Whitman and his three companions as she crossed a small bridge and vanished from sight. As many as eight other persons would later state that they saw a girl resembling Paula Welden in the area where she encountered the Whitman party. Within an hour of Whitman's sighting, the sun had set, and several hours later it began snowing. By Monday morning that area of the Long Trail was covered by three inches of snow over a bed of ice.

Paula Welden did not return to her room in Dewey Hall that Sunday night. When she didn't show up for her Monday morning classes, Elizabeth Johnson notified Bennington director of personnel Mary Garrett that she was missing, and the search for her began immediately. After marshaling all the resources of the college community to aid in the search, Bennington College president Lewis Webster Jones contacted Bennington County state's attorney William Travers Jerome Jr. A few hours later, Paula's father, W. Archibald Welden, arrived in town, and by the end of the day the search for Paula Welden had begun snowballing into a statewide and ultimately multistate manhunt. By the end of the week there were nearly a hundred newspaper reporters and photographers in Bennington to provide news about the case to an avid national public.

As with many missing-person cases, such as the initial search for Orville Gibson, the hunt for Paula Welden was hampered at first by uncertainty as to what had happened. Had she had an accident while hiking, and was she now lying helpless, injured, in a coma or dead in a remote snowdrift on the Long Trail? Was she suffering from amnesia, wandering who knows where, without knowledge of her own identity? Had she met foul play, been kidnapped, assaulted, or even murdered by someone she had met as she walked north into the Sunday night gloom? Or had Paula Welden orchestrated her own disappearance, with or without the assistance of others? And, if so, had she deliberately sought death in the killing winter wilderness of the Green Mountains—or had she cunningly created a false trail so that she could escape to a new life, with or without a romantic interest?

Lawmen investigating Paula's disappearance initially discounted foul play as a likely scenario. While search parties of Bennington and Williams College students and faculty organized for a thorough search of the Long Trail, state's attorney Jerome and Bennington police chief Francis J. Cone focused on running down the few available clues. Although Paula's clothing and apparent lack of funds suggested that she intended to return to her dormitory room, officials methodically investigated reports that she might have engineered her own disappearance. All Vermont Transit drivers who had piloted buses out of the Bennington bus terminal on Sunday were closely questioned, as were all Bennington taxi drivers. Such interrogations yielded nothing significant, although taxi driver Abe Ruskin identified a photograph of Paula as resembling a girl he had driven to the bus station on Sunday. But investigation of the buses she might have taken—a run to Pittsfield, Massachusetts, and a run to Albany, New York—proved fruitless. State's attorney Jerome acutely summarized police difficulties when he stated, "It looks as though we have a tough problem in this case, because we have no 'take off' point and we can't search the whole Green Mountain district."

Nevertheless, the hunt for Paula Welden soon did encompass much of the mountainous and even desolate terrain of the Long Trail area between Glastenbury and Bald Mountains. By Wednesday, December 4, there were as many as five hundred searchers looking for Paula along the Long Trail, some of them assisted by experienced woodsmen and accompanied by bloodhounds. Not a single significant clue was found, however, although police did identify about two dozen persons who might have seen Paula between the time she left her dorm room and was spotted by Ernie Whitman's group. Some footprints, too, were discovered by motorists Dan Murphy and his wife on a mountain road leading from Woodford Hollow toward Brattleboro. Similar footprints were discovered about a mile away by Mrs. Archie Barbeau near her home. But they were too indistinct to determine whether they were made by Paula Welden's shoes. On Thursday, December 5, ground searchers were joined by seven Marine Corps airplanes, whose pilots conducted wide-ranging searches of the Long Trail region. They were joined a day later by a helicopter, whose use and pilot were offered gratis by the Bell Aircraft Company. All searchers gave special scrutiny to the Everett Cave area on Mount Anthony, as Paula had once mentioned to Elizabeth Johnson that she wanted to go there. But no promising clue was turned up in any of these areas.

Owing in part to Vermont's paucity of law-enforcement resources, the search for Paula Welden soon expanded into a regional affair. Vermont had no state police force in 1946. Periodic efforts had been made over the previous decades to institute such a force, but they were continually stymied by local sheriffs jealous of their authority and the reluctance of thrifty state legislators to spend money on such a seeming frill. State of Vermont officials now did as much as they could, offering the assistance of state detective Almo B. Franzoni on the sixth day of the search. And flyers containing Paula's photograph and description went out by the hundreds to officials in New York, Massachusetts, New Hampshire, Connecticut, and Maine. The mounting publicity, fanned by newspapers and radio stations, alerted thousands of New Englanders to the hunt for Paula and broadcast her description throughout the entire United States.

As always, such widely broadcast appeals for information yielded some unwelcome results. It wasn't long before bogus sightings of the missing girl began to pour into state's attorney Jerome's office. The most sensational claim was that of Ora Telletier, a waitress at the Modern Restaurant in Fall River, Massachusetts. At 1 AM, December 5, that city's police chief, John McMahon, notified Bennington officials that Telletier had seen Paula Welden with a young man in her restaurant the day after she disappeared. Telletier recalled that the man had been abusively drunk and that the woman with him, who resembled Paula, had seemed dazed and unhappy. More significantly, the young woman had asked Telletier how far it was to Bennington and confided that she had arrived in Fall River that morning with $1,000 and didn't know what had become of it. Telletier's tale dominated the investigation for several days before police identified the man and woman she had served at the restaurant. The woman was not Paula, nor was it likely Paula who was reported to have been seen as she emerged from a railroad station in Boston on the night she disappeared. Other sightings, likewise exploded, had Paula spotted as she crossed the Canadian border at various points or was seen checking into various New England and New York State hotels and motels. A railroad conductor in New Haven, Connecticut, claimed to have seen a girl resembling Paula on a train bound for Charleston, South Carolina. All such clues came to nothing.

Meanwhile, the efforts of Vermont police sleuths were turning up seemingly more substantial, if ultimately frustrating, clues. Investigators spent much time running down and identifying three servicemen spotted by camper William Lauson on the Long Trail near the Glastenbury fire tower on Sunday afternoon. They were eventually found, questioned, and exonerated. And there were persistent reports that witnesses on the Long Trail had seen a maroon automobile with Connecticut license plates driving south on a road parallel to the trail. One of the witnesses was Woodford Hollow resident W. H. Myers, who recalled that the car contained a man and a woman who somewhat resembled Paula. Police also began searching for a half-ton truck with New York plates that had been seen in the area on Sunday. Like the maroon-colored car, this clue came to nothing.

Paula's father was intensely involved with the search for his daughter from the moment he arrived in Bennington. Displaying at all times an almost eerily stoic demeanor, he joined in the ground search for his daughter and administered the growing reward fund offered for information leading to the discovery of his daughter dead or alive. Nor did Mr. Welden spurn more desperate and outré efforts to find his daughter. On Wednesday, December 4, on the advice of some Vermont residents, he contacted Clara Jepson, a celebrated clairvoyant residing in Pownal. She informed him that Paula had walked through a covered bridge and then along the banks of a river for some distance. Jepson assured Welden that his daughter would be found alive in an old shack. Welden methodically searched the probable area along the Walloomsac River but found no trace of his daughter. Some days later, Mr. Welden received a letter from a New Hampshire clairvoyant, who informed him that Paula's body would be found in a cave near the "top of a mountain." Elmas Dicranian, a Pittsfield, Massachusetts, medium, also volunteered the tip that Paula's body had been left in a cemetery off U.S. Route 7. Authorities eventually identified the cemetery but found no trace of Paula there. More interestingly, a Mrs. Champaign, a seer of South Hero, told police details of her dream about

Paula. She said that the girl had met a man in a black automobile on the Long Trail. He had invited her into his camp for a cup of tea, attacked and murdered her, then buried her body underneath the floor of his camp. Although police did not think enough of Champaign's claim to publicize it at the time, they were able to identify a Long Trail camp belonging to Fred Gaudette as similar to the one described by Champaign. But Gaudette had an ironclad alibi for the afternoon of December 1.

With no real progress in the case apparent, the hitherto unruffled solidarity in the ranks of the Paula Welden searchers began to crack on the eighth day of her disappearance. The rift was triggered by state detective Franzoni's announcement, at a press conference on Monday night, December 9, that he was withdrawing from the case. His statement announcing his resignation was a concise summary of both the ambiguities of Paula's disappearance and Vermont's inability to deal with such a challenging case:

> Vermont has no state police force and no official agency designed to cope with this type of case. Unless we can prove a crime has been committed the state will have to relegate Miss Welden's case to the files of missing persons. My men and I are in this practically on a volunteer basis. We just don't have the authority to continue. We've tracked down every indication of foul play and we've run up again a blank wall on every lead.

Franzoni's bleakly frank statement blew the mask off the hitherto almost unnaturally composed W. Archibald Welden. He had up to this point been preternaturally patient with police officials and inquisitive reporters, even after they had publicly censured him for leaving Bennington to conduct his own, private two-day search for Paula, a grueling marathon of chasing down zany psychics, ephemeral rumors, and house-by-house interviews in the Long Trail region. But now, with a distraught wife at home in a state of utter collapse, and faced with the prospect of the Vermont cops pulling the plug, he understandably lost his patience in front of the reporters gathered in state's attorney Jerome's living room. After listening to Franzoni's explanation for closing the investigation, he icily asked aloud, "Just what have the state authorities done to find my daughter?" He then answered his own question: "I know the police have done all in their limited power to find Paula, but Vermont has a definite lack of police facilities for handling this type of case, and something should be done about it. The parents of every girl in Vermont face the same situation in which I now find myself should their daughter disappear."

With his daughter's fate at stake, Welden didn't content himself with angry public rhetoric. The following morning he drove to Arlington, where he poured out his heart to Dorothy Canfield Fisher, a national celebrity and well-known Vermont author. After listening to his plea for help, Fisher telephoned Vermont governor Mortimer B. Proctor and gave him an earful. The upshot was that on Tuesday evening Proctor ordered Vermont attorney general Alban J. Parker to request investigative aid from neighboring states and the Federal Bureau of Investigation. FBI officials in Albany, New York, quickly ruled out any participation in the search, stating that it was not within their jurisdiction. More helpfully, Connecticut commissioner of state police Edward J. Hickey offered the indefinite services of two crack missing-person sleuths, Lieutenants Robert Rundle and Dora C. Scoville. Both of them had impressive professional experience in missing-person cases, and the duo was already on the job in Bennington by Thursday, December 12. It seems probable, however, that the two Nutmeg State sleuths may have immediately ruffled the feathers of Vermont authorities with some unguarded and seemingly contemptuous comments on the prior efforts of their Green Mountain peers. On his very first day in Vermont, Rundle opined: "We're going back to the beginning and start the investigation from scratch. We've looked over most of the data gathered to date and we're convinced most of the so-called clues and leads are worthless—as they stand now, anyway."

Working the same invidious vein, his colleague Scoville added: "Of course, there's a lead waiting to be picked up somewhere, but I think we'll have to go a long way back to find it. A lot of possibilities may have been overlooked."

Whatever their hopes and expertise, Rundle and Scoville soon encountered the same frustrating bafflement as their Vermont colleagues. After talking with virtually everyone who might have seen Paula on December 1 and rechecking every lead and rumor in the case, they had made no progress whatsoever. Indeed, at the Sunday evening press conference, just three days after Rundle and Scoville entered the case, state's attorney Jerome confessed to reporters that all clues in the case had been "washed out."

There were a few more spectacular eruptions of rumor and supposition in the case. A fifteen-year-old Bennington girl created a stir when she told police she had been abducted by two men while walking in the Bennington area on the night of November 30, two days before Paula disappeared. The girl claimed that she had been seized, blindfolded, and taken on a fifteen-minute ride to a house. There, she had been presented to an unidentified woman, who said, "This is not the right girl. Take her back where you found her." Alas, the story evaporated under police interrogation, the girl finally admitting that she made it up because she feared the consequences of coming home late.

A similarly ephemeral sensation was the tale of a Rutland hotel employee, who told of a man in a black sedan who had stayed at the hotel on December 1. Flashing a large roll of cash and a revolver, the man had boasted he was en route to Bennington to keep a date with a "beautiful blonde." The story collapsed on investigation, but only after an eight-state alarm for the man's car and its alleged occupant had been broadcast.

Paula's father and police investigators had initially leaned toward the theories that Paula had either had an incapacitating accident on the Long Trail or met with foul play there. Inevitably, however, as the searchers became increasingly frustrated, the focus began to shift to Paula Welden herself and the possibility that she might have contrived her own disappearance. Her father insisted that she had generally seemed happy and that her most recent letters home had been characteristically cheerful. But roommate Elizabeth Johnson told investigators a different story, stating Paula had seemed depressed and emotionally upset during the week before she vanished. The *Bennington Banner* reported that a Bennington College employee claimed to have seen Paula weeping with a letter in her hand on Thanksgiving evening. On the other hand, some of Paula's college chums stated that she had seemed unusually happy at the party on November 30. Any of these stories, however contradictory, might fuel suspicions that her possible involvement with a man could have provoked her disappearance. As early as December 6 Bennington College president Jones was quoted as saying, "I'm convinced she planned her own disappearance." Archibald Welden was unwilling to fully embrace such a notion, but he did tell reporters at that same news conference, "I feel certain Paula must have left here—either of her own accord or under duress." But state's attorney Jerome well articulated the arguments against a voluntary disappearance at his Friday evening news conference on December 6. Noting that Paula evidently had little or no money with her and was not appropriately dressed for a prolonged hike on the Long Trail, he reasoned, "She was not the type of girl who would go on an extended trip with only a few dollars or dressed as informally as she was." There remained the possibility that she had arranged a rendezvous on the Long Trail or elsewhere, but there simply wasn't enough evidence to support such a theory. And the final word debunking Paula's possible complicity in her disappearance belonged to state detective Franzoni, who gave his estimate of Paula in his final report on the case, dated January 8, 1947: "I am at a loss to have to report that to date I cannot find a good motive. Paula Welden's life was checked and I can say she was a girl of good habits, a good scholar, but easily hurt and had few boyfriends. On the contrary she was of the type who would not hurt the feelings of others."

Hardly a girl, in short, to create the hurricane of anguish occasioned by her disappearance.

The only promising clue to emerge as the second week of the Welden search began was the report of a brown-red automobile—possibly the same as the mysterious maroon car—in the Glastenbury area of the Long Trail on Sunday evening, December 1. Camper Rose Michaels had seen the car and had become suspicious when she noticed its occupants were shining a light into the woods. She got a better look at the car on Monday morning, but she couldn't see its license plate. Elnora France, who lived near the Fay Fuller camp, had also seen the red-brown car. She had had to pull her dog out of its way as it passed, and she got close enough to see that it contained a dog and a "good-looking blonde." Interestingly, this automobile was eventually traced to Duanesburg, New York, where it had been stripped and set afire. But nothing more about it or its occupants was ever learned. Indeed, there were so many December 1 sightings of attractive blondes on the Long Trail that authorities eventually concluded that there might have been several blondes there—none of whom was necessarily Paula

Welden. Indeed, the haziness of some of the identifications raised the possibility that Paula had never even made it to the Long Trail.

The hunt ground on, producing a few ephemeral clues and mounting frustration. While searching along Route 9 on Monday afternoon, December 9, some sleuth found a pair of bloodstained pink panties lying in the thick brush. But Elizabeth Johnson and Bennington director of personnel Mary Garret were certain that they didn't belong to Paula. Investigators were briefly hopeful when word came from Northampton, Massachusetts, that police there were holding a man who had attacked a Smith College student. But police quickly ruled out any connection between the man and Paula's disappearance. There was more sustained interest in the tale of a Bennington girl who told a *Banner* reporter that she had been dating a man named Raymond. She said Raymond told her that on December 1 he had picked up a hitchhiker named Paula, who had told him she was bored and wanted to go to the movies. He had dropped her off at the Stark Theater in downtown Bennington and never seen her again. Although Raymond's girl couldn't even remember his last name, investigators eventually tracked him down and eliminated him as a suspect.

As the second week of the search ground on, the lack of progress in the investigation began to take its toll on the so-far unflappable Lieutenant Rundle. Having reexamined every iota of information in the case and reinterviewed every known eyewitness, he found himself facing the same brick wall encountered by his less illustrious Vermont predecessors. On Friday, December 13, he finally vented his frustration, telling reporters, "A lot of people have confused this case by telling a lot of lies and half-truths." Rundle would not, however, identify just who had told him lies or half-truths. His partner Scoville also commented in the same key, angrily complaining about the letters, anonymous or otherwise, that had "cluttered" their investigation with crackpot notions and wild allegations.

There was more indication that same Friday that the official investigation into Paula's disappearance had just about run its course. That afternoon the *Bennington Banner* published a letter from W. Archibald Welden, publicly thanking the administration, faculty, and students of Bennington College for their help in trying to find his daughter. Two days later, as Bennington's churches rang their bells in unison to inaugurate the Christmas season, Paula's father packed up her personal belongings and left for his home in Stamford. He told state's attorney Jerome he wouldn't be back unless there was a significant break in the case. He did, however, return later that week to finalize the details of the reward offer and to thank the people of Bennington for their support. His reward announcement offered $5,000 to anyone finding Paula alive and $2,000 to anyone finding her body. By that time it was clear that the latest hot lead in the case had failed: Noticing that there had been a landslide at a seventy-five-foot-deep gravel pit near the Bennington campus, local game warden Jesse Warden suggested the possibility that Paula had wandered to the pit on Sunday afternoon and been buried by the collapsing material. It took a steam shovel several hours to remove the 450 cubic yards of earth—but searchers found no Paula Welden underneath. Meanwhile, it was reported that Elizabeth Johnson, harassed by two weeks of interrogation, had suffered a nervous breakdown and was being treated in the Bennington infirmary.

Lieutenants Rundle and Scoville had stated on Friday, December 20, that they would stay on the case "indefinitely." Three days later, however, they threw in the towel and returned to Connecticut. At the press conference announcing their withdrawal, state's attorney Jerome aptly summarized the state of the investigation: "As it stands now, the investigation is at an absolute standstill because of a lack of clues. After twenty-three days of searching we know little if anything that we did not know the day Miss Welden dropped out of sight."

Publicly admitting defeat, Rundle added, "We know Miss Welden is supposed to have left the campus to go for a walk on Glastenbury Mountain, and that's all we know. Some people think they saw her en route to the mountain, but some people also reported seeing her at widely scattered points throughout New England."

Meanwhile, W. Archibald Welden was back in Stamford, preparing for a grim family Christmas. The night before Rundle and Scoville pulled out of the case, he broadcast a message to his missing daughter over radio station WSTC in Stamford. Although he now leaned toward the theory that she had been abducted, his desperate radio plea also embraced the possibility that she had vanished of her own free will:

> Paula, in just two more days it will be Christmas. If you can hear me, know that we love you and want you. Whatever may have prompted you to leave us, if you have gone off on your own free will, be sure we will find a better answer to your problem by working it out together. Just pick up the nearest telephone and ask for me. You won't need change. The operator will reverse the charges. I will come immediately. Lots of love from us all.

And that was pretty much the end of the Paula Welden search, if not its enduring mystery. Heavy winter snowfalls soon hindered access to the Long Trail area where she had likely disappeared. Five months later, more than a hundred volunteers returned to the region, searching twenty-four square miles of the wooded mountains for traces of Paula before giving up. Echoes of the Welden case continued for a few years, each one eliciting brief interest before coming to nothing. A headless corpse found in the Winooski River in July

1947 provoked a flurry of excitement before it was proved to be the body of a man. In December 1948 Vermont state detectives journeyed to Massachusetts to question twenty-three-year-old art student Carl Rockel, who had been arrested for viciously slashing a man during a Cambridge street robbery. Police had found a clipping about the Welden case in his wallet and a sketch resembling Paula in his room. Rockel admitted having once been in the Glastenbury Mountain Long Trail area, but authorities could not find any connection with Paula's disappearance. The Welden case also resurfaced the following year, when James Tetford disappeared from his bus seat on the third anniversary of the Welden vanishing.

Meanwhile, behind the scenes, Vermont authorities had reconsidered the foul-play scenario, specifically the Long Trail murder-burial theory offered by South Hero psychic Mrs. W. Champaign. On August 28, 1947, Albert B. Christie, a Vermont state investigator working on the Welden case, and Bennington County state's attorney James Stuart Holden went to Windsor Prison to interview inmate Lloyd Wilkins. Wilkins told a lurid tale, allegedly related to him that summer by fellow prisoner Terrance Stone. Christie subsequently sent this summary of Wilkins's narrative to Vermont commissioner of public safety Merritt A. Edson:

> Wilkins stated that Stone said he had killed a girl and buried her underneath the floor of a camp—had covered up her body and relaid the floor. Stone further stated to Wilkins that he had known Paula Welden when she was 15 years old when he lived in a rooming house in Connecticut. Stone further stated to Wilkins that he had a camp on the Long Trail outside Bennington and had done considerable hunting on the Trail.

Both Christie and Holden were convinced that Wilkins was lying, convinced he had fabricated his sensational story in hopes of having his sentence for the rape of a ten-year-old child reduced. They didn't even bother to interview Stone—but they were intrigued enough by Wilkins's account to send photographs of Stone to W. Archibald Welden. Welden told Christie and Holden that he didn't recognize the man and that he didn't believe the convict had ever known Paula, and the matter was subsequently dropped. On September 13, 1952, Bennington County state's attorney John B. Harte officially closed his office's investigation into the Welden disappearance.

Journalist Mary Baillie, who wrote a speculative series about the Welden mystery in the *Bennington Banner* during the fall of 2000, is probably correct that the Champaign/Stone Long Trail murder-burial scenario deserved more scrutiny than it was given at the time. This author is disinclined to give credence to the paranormal origins of Mrs. Champaign's scenario—but it *is* eerily disquieting how much her psychic vision and the alleged Stone confession agree in their details. In any case, the likelihood that Paula met with foul play seems just as probable as the theories she met with an accident or decided to find a new identity and life. Her body, forgotten and unknown, may very well lie beneath the floor of one of the many camps along the Long Trail. But despite repeated and intensive searches of the relevant terrain, no trace of her has ever been found, nor has intensive probing of her life and personality revealed anything that might have motivated her to pull a vanishing act. And the fact that she wasn't properly dressed for a long mountain hike, plus the presumption that she didn't have much money with her, strongly indicates one of two possibilities: 1) that she intended to return soon to her room; or 2) she had plans to meet someone on the Long Trail. As the latter scheme seems inconsistent with the known facts of her personality, the strongest remaining hypothesis is that she met a lethal stranger up on the Long Trail.

A popular current theory about the fate of Paula Welden is the

"Bennington Triangle" concept popularized in 1994 by Vermont mystery maven Joseph Citro in his book, *Green Mountain Ghosts, Ghouls & Unsolved Mysteries*. Citing a number of well-known, unsolved disappearances in the Bennington area, Citro focused on five in particular to buttress his theory that something uncanny was going on in the region. In addition to Paula Welden, he considered:

- Middie Rivers, a seventy-four-year-old woodsman who disappeared on November 12, 1945, while leading a party of hunters in the same area where Paula Welden was last seen.

- James Tetford, the World War I veteran who vanished from a Bennington-bound bus on December 1, 1949.

- Paul Jepson, an eight-year-old North Bennington boy who vanished from the town dump between 3 and 4 PM on October 12, 1950.

- Freida Langer, a fifty-three-year-old, seasoned outdoorswoman who disappeared while camping in the Glastenbury Mountain region. Her body eventually turned up near the Somerset Reservoir seven months later—but the cause of her death could not be determined, and officials were at a loss to explain why her body had not been previously found in the intensively searched area.

Citro had a lot of fun with his spooky catalog of the disappeared, ultimately culminating his suspenseful accounts with a fusillade of playfully rhetorical questions about the fate of his unfortunate subjects:

Could the Bennington Monster have carried them off into the caves and swamps of Glastenbury Mountain? Could they have slipped through some vile vortex, some interdimensional trap door like the one referred to as the Bermuda Triangle, famous for gobbling up planes and ships that are never seen again? Or maybe they encountered an enchanted stone known to the Indians as one that yawns and swallows anyone who steps on it?

A whimsical set of hypotheses, to be sure, but nary a one that brings us any closer to a sensible solution of the Paula Welden mystery. This author suspects, however, that supporters of the Bennington Triangle theory might be more skeptical of such bizarre explanations if they were better acquainted with similar disappearances in many of the other forty-nine states. Quite a few persons have disappeared without a trace throughout the United States over the past two centuries, and a surprising number of college students, usually female, have likewise vanished. (For a case very similar to the Welden mystery, see the author's narrative of the 1937 disappearance of Ohio Wesleyan University undergraduate Ruth Baumgardner in "The Vanishing Coed," *Death Ride At Euclid Beach: And More True Tales of Crime And Disaster From Cleveland's Past*; Gray & Co. Publishers, 2004.) This is an enormous country, and even in our contemporary "global village" of instant and omnipresent communications, it is still possible, as the volume of cases at the Vermont Department of Public Safety attests, to disappear "without a trace."

It has now been over sixty years since Paula Welden vanished, and no new evidence has appeared since then, except Mary Baillie's disclosure of the Champaign/Wilkins scenarios, which were not publicized when originally voiced. And there is no reason to give any credence to Baillie's odious flirtation with the obscene notion that Paula's father did away with her: "An opinion is forwarded that perhaps, just perhaps, W. Archibald Welden was out in the woods, alone with a shovel . . . burying the body of his beautiful daughter!"

And so the Paula Welden case remains as it was on December 2,

1946: an endlessly repetitive "Groundhog Day" in which every clue comes to naught and every search rebounds upon itself. But the Welden tragedy did have one positive outcome. As a result of criticism of Vermont's law enforcement resources leveled by W. Archibald Welden and others involved in the case, the Vermont legislature passed Act No. 163, which created the Vermont Department of Public Safety, the Green Mountain State's first statewide police force. After years of opposition by local sheriffs and budget-conscious politicians, it became a reality on July 1, 1947, just seven months after Paula Welden disappeared. Paula Welden, *requiescat in pace.*

CHAPTER 11

DEATH OF AN ANARCHIST

The 1903 Killing of Eli Corti

> Very few things happen at the right time, and the rest do not happen at all. The conscientious historian will correct these defects.
>
> —Herodotus

Historical truth is an elusive goal. While history may not be "a set of lies agreed upon," as Napoleon's cynical phase would have it, it is frequently difficult, if not impossible, to reconstruct the reality of past events with accuracy or impartiality. For the past *is* past—and what survives as evidence or testimony of men's deeds is often arbitrary, equivocal, or ambiguous. And the difficulties of ascertaining the truth of historical events are even more challenging when such events involve a crime or tragedy. Human beings are ever fallible, forgetful, and liable to distort or alter their recollections of their most mundane and inconsequential actions. But they are even more likely to do so when the stakes are greater, as when they are participants or witnesses in violent and criminal events. An illustrative example on a global scale is the Turkish government's near century-long denial that it orchestrated the genocide of as many as 1.5 million Armenians between 1915 and 1922. Despite the existence of persuasive physical and archival evidence and damning eyewitness testimony, millions of persons—many of them honest people of goodwill—still disagree on what happened to all those Armenians and who was really to blame. So, too, it is with smaller-scale and local events. Consider, for example, the story of Eli Corti's killing, a seemingly well-publicized Vermont episode about which we may never know the full truth.

Contemporary Barre, Vermont, does not exactly suggest visions of Deadwood, South Dakota, circa 1876. For whatever its incivilities, present-day Barre is hardly a "wide-open" social cauldron of hot-headed young gunslingers, literally lethal political warfare, and inhumanly exploitive industrial misery. Yet just a century ago Barre *was* a brawling, frontier-style industrial town, with all the problems endemic to such settlements. Like Deadwood and other western mining towns, it had a dynamic mining industry employing thousands of young men, most of them working in dangerous and unhealthy circumstances. And as in Deadwood, the destabilizing effects of explosive industrial expansion and population growth were exacerbated by tensions between the disparate groups drawn to the area by its economic boom. But unlike Deadwood, with its Chinese and Native American contingents, Barre's social fissures were along ethnic, rather than blatantly racial, lines. The real conflicts developed with the arrival of the Italians, beginning in the late 1880s and surging to a flood tide of immigrants in the 1890s.

It is difficult to make generalizations about the several thousand Italians who settled in Barre as the nineteenth century ebbed away. There is much evidence that the established Vermonters, predominately of Anglo-Saxon stock, lumped all the new Italian arrivals together as quaintly picturesque, if sometimes threatening, foreigners of unintelligible speech and inferior culture. (Such patronizing indifference was frequently evidenced by the fact that Vermont newspapers of the day, such as the *Montpelier Evening Argus* and the *Barre Daily Times*, habitually garbled the spelling of Italian names, frequently misidentifying even prominent figures in the immigrant community.) But as journalist Robin Ray has noted, the Italians who came to Barre were largely literate and skilled stone carvers from northern Italy, unlike the often illiterate and relatively unskilled Italians who settled in large cities like New York, Philadelphia, and Cleveland. These skilled artisans, mostly from the the Carrara, Lake Como, Varese, and Viggiù regions, brought their craft with them and gradually displaced the immigrant Scots carvers who had previously dominated the Barre stone-carving industry.

The Italian carvers brought more to their new Vermont homes than their almost superhuman talents for fashioning marble and granite into perdurable, solid poetry. They also brought with them their political convictions, which took root and quickly blossomed for better or ill in the harsh squalor of the booming Barre mine area. Most of the politically conscious Italian immigrants were united in their loathing for the existing Italian monarchy and the Roman Catholic Church. What differences remained, however, eventually crystallized into the rival formation of anarchist and socialist factions as the twentieth century began. As with most leftist quarrels of the era, the main ideological split was over the question of direct action, the anarchists embracing the immediate overthrow of existing political institutions and the socialists leaning toward gradualist reform and a distaste for the violent "propaganda of the deed" exemplified by such anarchist actions as the 1901 assassination of President William McKinley. The acrimony between the two groups steadily worsened throughout the late 1890s, perhaps, as Henry Kissinger once observed of faculty politics, because their differences were actually so minuscule. But worsen they did, although some of the anarchists helped in the erection of the socialists' Labor Hall on Granite Street, which opened to a packed audience of almost seven hundred persons on November 28, 1900. It soon proved its usefulness, serving as a convenient facility for dances, fund-raisers, and an adjunct cooperative store.

Ironically enough, the opening of the Labor Hall also helped precipitate a political explosion between the socialists and anarchists and an act of shocking violence. One month after the opening, on the night of December 27, Barre police chief Patrick Brown paid a visit to the hall. Warned that violence was in the offing, he and his officers eventually closed down the dance in progress there and suppressed several potential fights. Revenge was swift in coming. At 3:00 the following morning, Chief Brown was surprised by a group of men as he emerged from a doorway while making his rounds in downtown Barre. At least one of them fired two bullets into him, both of which hit him in the abdomen. Miraculously, his life was saved when one of the bullets was partially deflected by one of his uniform buttons.

The shooting proved a wake-up call to Barre's non-Italian citizens, who hadn't previously paid much attention to the obscure political squabbles of the town's newest immigrant community. But despite the fact that many Italians were "rousted" by the Barre police in the ensuing investigation and ten of them indicted by a Washington County grand jury, the ultimate consequences of the shooting were less than might have been expected by the initial furor it provoked. On May 10, 1901, Judge John H. Watson sentenced anarchist Arturo Barnacci (sometimes rendered as *Bernaco*) to twenty-five years in Windsor Prison for shooting Chief Brown, and several of Barnacci's accomplices were convicted on lesser charges.

Barnacci's lawyer, Fred L. Laird, argued in defense of his client, with some plausibility, that Barnacci had merely been drunk and had not intended to kill Chief Brown. Whatever the truth, it is unmistakable that the Barre socialists exploited the shooting to score publicity points against the anarchists. Two days after the shooting, a delegation of prominent socialists visited Chief Brown in his hospital bed. Thanking him for breaking up the Wednesday night dance fracas, they asserted that his timely intervention had prevented a veritable bloodbath. Indeed, they insisted, Chief Brown had unknowingly frustrated a meticulously planned anarchist conspiracy to assassinate thirteen previously targeted socialists there when a prearranged signal was given. The socialists followed up this never-verified bombshell by presenting Barre authorities with a list containing the names of every supposed anarchist in the area.

Relations between Barre's socialists and anarchists deteriorated further during the next two years. One likely factor was the radical polarization of American opinion about anarchism triggered by the assassination of President McKinley by anarchist Leon Czolgosz in Buffalo on September 6, 1901. Most Americans were horrified by McKinley's murder, and the ensuing popular hostility to anarchism also encouraged socialists, who did not want to be tarred with the same terrorist brush, to put even more political distance between themselves and anarchism. (A telling index of American antipathy to anarchists is furnished by the ship-passengers lists of arriving immigrants required by U.S. law in the early 1900s: Questions asked included whether the passenger was an anarchist or polygamist.)

Not that American hostility to anarchism crimped the style of Barre's lively adherents. Amazingly, it so thrived there in this period that even as late as 1908 the *New York Times* characterized Barre's anarchist community as second in importance only to that of Paterson, New Jersey. Indeed, that same newspaper stated almost admiringly, "It is said that the leaders [of Paterson] use the quiet granite town as a place of refuge when the police of New Jersey get too hot upon the trail." Anarchist convictions so flourished in Barre that by the time of the Eli Corti killing in 1903, there were at least five hundred subscribers to anarchist publications in that town.

Things heated up considerably with the arrival of Luigi Galleani in June of that year. An influential twentieth-century anarchist, Galleani was an unapologetic advocate for the overthrow of the U.S. government and would later become notorious when his newspaper *Cronaca Sovversiva* (Subversive Chronicle) was suppressed by the federal government during World War I. (Galleani also deserves a footnote in history for publishing articles in his newspaper by two other Italian anarchists, Nicola Sacco and Bartolomeo Vanzetti.) He came to Barre that summer from Canada, which had expelled him after he fled a New Jersey indictment for inciting to riot. Commencing the publication of *Cronaca Sovversiva,* he soon filled its columns with vituperation of socialists, both in Barre and the wider world. Steeped in anticlericalism and a hatred of all police organizations, he particularly delighted, as did his fellow anarchist journalists and orators, in denouncing his socialist adversaries as "spies," "fakirs," and "priests."

Galleani's abuse soon stimulated opponents worthy of his enmity. The most prominent was Giacinto Menotti Serrati, an Italian journalist who would eventually become a leader of the Italian Communist Party in the 1920s. But at the turn of the century he was yet a socialist, and he battled Galleani and other anarchists both in the columns of his influential New York City newspaper, *Il Proletario,* and in public forums. One such confrontation came in Barre on May 2, 1902, when Serrati came to Barre's new Labor Hall to debate Galleani on the question, "Which Would Be Better for the Italian People: Anarchism or Socialism?"

By the autumn of 1903, relations between Barre socialists and anarchists were again dangerously toxic, a situation aggravated by the intemperate abuse dished out in Serrati and Galleani's respective newspapers. That September, Serrati repeatedly insulted the Barre anarchists in print, calling them "ruffians," "counterfeiters" [that is, fakirs], and "liars." Galleani responded in kind, working in concert with the editors of other anarchist newspapers, such as San Francisco's *Protesta Umana* and Paterson's *Questione Sociale,* to characterize Serrati as a "usurer," "editor-speculator," "dirty personage," and "spy." Such words may seem mere juvenile posturing to present-day Americans, but to the proud Barre anarchists and socialists they were fighting, even killing, words. By the first week of October both sides were itching for a fight, and it was Serrati himself who now provided the pretext.

Serrati's decision to speak in Barre was not provocative per se. As noted, he had spoken there before and was well known to both political factions. So there was nothing unusual or particularly calculated in his decision to speak publicly in Barre about his current feud with the anarchists. We may take him at his word that he simply wanted to clear the air, especially as he was about to leave for Europe to confer with fellow moguls in the world socialist movement. He arrived in town on Friday, October 2, and by the next afternoon Barre was flooded with handbills announcing that he would speak that evening at 7:00 at the Labor Hall on "The Methods of Socialist Struggle."

From this point on in the narrative, it becomes impossible to be certain about what occurred at the Labor Hall that night. After the event, there were persistent suspicions, fervently believed by Barre socialists, that there was a secret anarchist plot to disrupt Serrati's lecture or worse. Labor historian and Barre's Aldrich Library director Karen Lane has cited as evidence of such a conspiracy, or at least the belief such a conspiracy existed, the reminiscence of Labor Hall director Peter Peroni that the Barre anarchists "made no secret of the fact that they intended to heckle and otherwise disrupt the talk." No anarchist, however, ever admitted to such a preconcerted purpose, and it was later denied under oath by several anarchist witnesses who were at the Labor Hall that night. Some of those same witnesses also categorically denied attending a meeting on the afternoon of October 3, at which such a disruption was allegedly planned. It seems probable, however, that some sort of scheme, formal or informal, was contrived by the Barre anarchists to make things at least rhetorically hot for Serrati that evening. Their hatred for him was almost palpable, with even the children of Barre's anarchists trained to jeer at him as a "spy" when he strolled the streets of town.

As in romance, timing is everything when it comes to the contingencies that produce murder. For reasons never adequately explained, G. M. Serrati did not show up in time for his lecture at the Labor Hall that Saturday night; 7 PM came and went, and fifteen more minutes elapsed as the audience became increasingly restive and impatient. More ominously, most of those in the crowd of thirty to forty-five persons in the second-floor meeting room were anarchists. As customary, Serrati's handbills had stated that his lecture was open to everyone, and Barre's anarchists had arrived in force, outnumbering the few socialists present by five or six to one.

Like a playground shoving match, the trouble started with petty insults and name-calling. By 7:15 it was obvious that the speaker was tardy, and some of the anarchists began gleefully baiting the handful of nervous socialists, focusing their taunts on Joseph Bernasconi. The most barbed taunts came from Luigi Cassi and Ferdinand Comi (a brother of Eli Corti's wife). "Where is the orator?" they jeered. "Where is the 'priest'? Where is your 'spy'?" An angry Bernasconi retorted, "Be patient, the speaker will come." A minute later, anarchist Martini Rizzi joined in the fun, taunting Bernasconi, "All you socialists are cowards. Why don't you summon the speaker with your church bell?"—an insult linking the socialists to the despised Catholic church. "We don't have a bell, but we could collect the money to buy one," replied Bernasconi. "If you want trouble, why don't you take it outside?"

The accounts of what happened next do not agree. By now anarchist Emilio Vochini had joined Rizzi in baiting Bernasconi. When Bernasconi refused to go outside, Vochini either grabbed him by the neck or Bernasconi slapped Vochini. Whatever happened, their encounter set off a general free-for-all, with perhaps a dozen anarchists pummeling the few socialists in the hall. As more and more punches were thrown, and more and more men joined in the fray, the room exploded into chaos. Knocked to the floor, Bernasconi writhed beneath of a heap of attackers, some of his assailants shouting, "Kill him! Pound him! Throw him out the window!" And as Martini Rizzi grappled with socialist Caesar Brussa (or Bruzzi), Vochini grabbed a chair and hit Brussa over the head, dropping him to the floor.

Some witnesses would later recall that the threats of the attacking anarchists now became more general, with shouts of "Kill them all! They are all fakirs and priests. Throw them out the window!"

The violence lasted but a few minutes and did not involve all the persons present. But one of them was thirty-five-year-old Barre socialist Alessandro Garetto. Employed by the firm of George Walker & Son, and living in a house at 108 Railroad Street, Garetto had a wife and four-year-old daughter. A tall, imposing man with a dark complexion, Garetto enjoyed the reputation of an industrious, sober workman. One of the earlier arrivals to the Labor Hall, Garetto had waited patiently for the speaker, sitting quietly in a chair and smoking a cigar. But as the fracas began to envelop the hall, he somehow became swept up in the fighting. He would always insist that he had been minding his own business when he was attacked and beaten by a group of anarchists. At least one reputed eyewitness, Rogini Cirillo, would later testify that he saw Garetto frantically struggling to get out of the room to escape the anarchists pounding him with their fists. On the other hand, several anarchist witnesses would claim that Garetto was never molested and that his path to the door to the stairway exit was open throughout the melee. But less partisan witnesses, including Barre policemen, would later attest that sometime that evening Garetto was badly beaten badly about his head, suffering injuries that required medical attention.

Was Eli Corti involved in the violence or, more specifically, the attack on Alessandro Garetto? There is nothing murkier in the Corti tragedy than the role of its central victim. Born in Viggiù, Italy, the birthplace of a thousand Barre stone workers, the ambitious Corti had learned his carving craft well before coming to the United States in 1891. A dutiful husband and father of three daughters, the new immigrant rose quickly to the top tier of area stone carvers. In 1898 he and master carver Samuel Novelli joined together in the firm of Novelli & Corti. Just a year later the two artisans achieved a stunning professional triumph, when they were chosen to execute the carving on the Robert Burns statue in downtown Barre. Still standing today, the statue of Burns created by Novelli and the base panels carved by Corti depicting scenes from Burns's poems remain as enduring testaments of their virtuoso skills in stone.

There was another side, however, to industrious, soft-spoken, family man Eli Corti. Although some of his friends would later publicly deny it, he brought his anarchist political convictions with him to the United States. Indeed, although his partisans liked to describe him as entirely apolitical, he was in fact politically committed enough to serve for a while as the secretary of the Barre anarchist group.

That said, Corti's friends and his anarchist brother William were probably telling the truth when they testified under oath that Eli Corti took little interest in politics after he graduated from the status of skilled artisan to small businessman in a successful carving firm. It was a natural enough process for an ambitious immigrant, and the process was later explicated somewhat cynically by an unknown *New York Times* correspondent in his analysis of the real animus between the Barre socialists and anarchists:

> [T]hose of the radicals who were skillful workmen grew very prosperous. When a few Socialists entered the Italian colony the richer Anarchists turned Socialists so generally as to suggest that with another generation and slightly larger bank accounts the original "reds" might be joining the hated capitalist class. At first the two parties clubbed together to build a new hall, but the greater wealth of the Socialists soon made itself felt. Their feasts were more splendid and the belles of the Socialists outdressed those of the Anarchists and the feud was on.

Whatever his politics, Eli Corti was indisputably present in the Labor Hall that night. It was never explained exactly why this allegedly apolitical man was present, although he might have been drawn to it simply as a family social event, since at least one of his brothers and several of his in-laws, all anarchist sympathizers, were also present. The accounts of his behavior that night do not agree. Some witnesses insisted that Corti tried to play the role of neutral peacemaker as the hot words escalated into physical violence. More than one spectator recalled him trying to calm the brawlers, repeatedly shouting, "Keep quiet!" with his arms stretched out in a pleading manner. Others, however, including socialist Louis Bruzza, remembered Corti as one of the mob who was enthusiastically beating Alessandro Garetto as he made frantic efforts to get out of the room.

At some point in the mounting violence Garetto panicked. The evidence is convincing that he was being beaten, voices were screaming that all the socialists should be killed, and fighters with knives were beginning to bring them into play. Martini Rizzi stabbed Caesar Brussa, already reeling from Vochini's attack with a chair, in the head, and others were wounded by flashing steel. Bleeding from his wound, Brussa staggered to his feet and stumbled out the door to the stairway exit, screaming, "Mama, Mama, the assassins are killing me!" As he left, he heard two gunshots.

Alessandro Garetto may have fired three shots. No one ever actually saw him fire at all, although anarchist Luigi Cassi testified that he saw Garetto make several moves toward his hip pocket, as if to draw a gun, before the actual shooting. Cassi claimed that he merely stared Garetto down each time, warning, "Look out, for I see you."

Notwithstanding the absence of eyewitnesses, there is no question that Garetto fired at least twice. Crazed by fear, he probably fired his initial shot at random, rather than aiming at any specific person. That shot, fired from about six feet away, hit Eli Corti in the abdomen. Taking a slightly downward path, the .32 caliber center-fire bullet penetrated Corti's vest, his blue flannel shirt and his undershirt, and smashed into his stomach, drilling holes in the front and rear before lodging in some muscles by his spinal column. Grasping his stomach in pain, Corti blurted, "I am shot! Right here! Right here! Send for a doctor," and collapsed backward to the floor.

Garetto's second shot was more deliberate. Hearing the first shot and seeing Garetto with a revolver, Emilio Vochini lurched toward him with the handy chair he had used to dispatch Caesar Brussa. Garetto fired at him but missed, the bullet passing between

Vochini's body and upper arm without inflicting more than a scratch. Turning to flee out the door, Garetto was confronted there by Joseph Movalli, who kicked him in the stomach. Falling backward, he tumbled down several steps of the staircase, where he lay too stunned to move for a few seconds. Recovering himself, Garetto limped down the stairs and ran down Granite Street in frantic fear of his expected pursuers.

Garetto must have been a sight as he raced north up Granite Street and turned west onto Summer Street, his head bleeding profusely as he ran. He turned south onto Elm Street and sprinted down to the municipal building and into the chambers of Barre city judge Allan C. Fay. Unaware of the shooting, Fay was somewhat baffled by the sudden appearance of the terrified, bleeding, and breathless man who now crouched cowering in his office. Garetto spoke little English, but Fay was eventually able to understand Garetto's assertion that the anarchists were trying to kill him. In lieu of better information, Fay decided to take him to the police station downstairs and have them sort the situation out.

Fay's action was a timely one. Already quite a number of angry Italians were roaming the Barre streets, looking for Alessandro Garetto with bloody vengeance in mind. Just minutes earlier, word had come to Police Chief Brown that there had been a shooting at the Labor Hall. So by the time Fay arrived at the station with Garetto in tow, Brown and all his officers had left in search of Garetto. The first lawmen to return were George Wood and Donald McPhee. Taking Garetto into custody, they first searched him, finding an unopened box of revolver cartridges. When asked where his revolver was, Garetto insisted that the anarchists had taken it from him. Despite strenuous efforts, the murder revolver was never located. To insure his safety, Brown stashed Garetto in the city lockup while he plotted measures to ensure his safety from lynch law.

Meanwhile, Eli Corti was fighting for his life. Removed from the floor of the Labor Hall, he was taken to the nearby house of Paul Minini. Barre physician F. C. Ligouri was the first doctor to reach his side, followed by Drs. Patrick E. McSweeney and Joseph W. Jackson. The latter two quickly confirmed Dr. Ligouri's grim diagnosis and prognosis. It was an ugly gunshot wound, virtually identical to the one that had killed President McKinley, an injury almost invariably fatal. Having done all they could, the physicians decided about 10 PM to remove Corti to Heaton Hospital for more heroic measures.

The trip to Montpelier in A. W. Badger & Co.'s ambulance furnished even more than the situation's expected drama. Fearing mob vengeance, Police Chief Brown had decided to send the accused shooter there, too, to the more secure confines of the county jail. Having already smuggled Garetto to a house on the outskirts of Montpelier, he now had the ambulance carrying Corti stop outside there. Garetto was then brought out and confronted by Eli Corti. As a policeman shone a lamp on Garetto's face, Corti stared at him and said twice, "You are the man who shot me."

The sight of the accused man was too much for Samuel Novelli, who had been allowed to ride in the ambulance with his wounded partner. Screaming, "You murderer!" he grabbed the lantern from the policeman and hurled it at Garetto's face. He missed, and the lantern hit Chief Brown in the head. The enraged Novelli then made a grab for Brown's police revolver, demanding that he be allowed to finish off Garetto right then and there. As Novelli was dragged away by police, the ambulance began the journey to Montpelier.

Despite the bleak prognosis, doctors at Heaton Hospital labored hard to save Corti's life. Probing for the bullet, Drs. Charles Chandler, M. F. McGuire, and William Lindsay removed and repaired his stomach. They could not find the bullet, however, so they simply replaced the stomach, and the family and friends of the wounded man settled into a death watch beside his hospital bed. Corti was conscious most of the time and conversed rationally, firmly stating his wishes as to his funeral and again identifying Alessandro Garetto as the man who shot him. At last, around midnight Sunday, almost thirty hours after the shooting, he expired as his grieving family and friends helplessly watched. The following morning, Washington County state's attorney Frank A. Bailey began preparations to try Garetto for murder and other Italians on miscellaneous riot and assault charges.

Eli Corti's funeral, held on the afternoon of October 6 in his Blackwell Street home, was a well-attended and moving spectacle. In accordance with his dying requests, there was no priest officiating or the customary Italian band playing. After the simple ceremony, an escort of fifty-two mourner-filled wagons accompanied his remains to their final destination in Hope Cemetery. Later, a group of his fellow carvers, including brother William Corti and brother-in-law John Comi, would create the stunning stone memorial that still adorns his grave. Once seen, it is never forgotten: Dressed in a suit and bow tie, Corti sits with his right knee bent, his right hand stroking his face, and his left hand on a pillar bearing his birth and death dates. At his feet lie his professional tools: a square, mallet, calipers, and pneumatic hammer.

Considering the politics and the ethnic divisions involved, the Garetto trial proved to be a remarkably fair and, perhaps more surprisingly, unsensational affair. An editorial in the *Rutland Daily Herald,* later reprinted in the *Montpelier Evening Argus,* well expressed the fearful attitudes of Vermont's native-born population toward the political turmoil disclosed by the Labor Hall riot:

Barre is infested with a gang of anarchists of the lower type—
the less intelligent—and is in imminent danger of repetitions
of these outbreaks unless this gang is thoroughly cleaned out or
taught respect for law and order. Whiskey and unintelligent anarchists are a dangerous combination: and Barre seems to have
just such a cancer on its body politic. The knife should be ap-
plied speedily and clear to the roots or the city will soon find itself delivered over entirely to a dangerous element.

Notwithstanding such draconian attitudes, the Garetto trial was
remarkably free from appeals to political or ethnic prejudice. But
there was another and utterly unavoidable problem, for in addition
to the possible prejudices Vermont jurors might entertain toward
Italians of leftist persuasion, the trial officials and jury members
also had to struggle with a formidable language barrier. Few of the
lawyers involved, much less the potential jurors, spoke or understood Italian, and many of the potential Italian witnesses to the
Labor Hall violence did not speak or understand English. But interpreters were speedily recruited, and a special grand jury began
hearing testimony in the case on October 13. After examining
ninety-four witnesses, it returned six indictments on the morning
of November 4. Two of them charged Garetto with murder, and the
remaining true bills indicted Joseph Bernasconi, Emilio Vochini,
Antonio Bianchi, and Vincenzo Crovella (or Crolla) on breach of
the peace charges for their part in the October 3 riot. Meanwhile,
Garetto remained in the county jail, not speaking to anyone on the
advice of his attorney, Fred L. Laird.

Laird fought hard to delay his client's day in court, arguing that
the community was so inflamed as to preclude a fair trial. But
Vermont Supreme Court justice Seneca Haselton agreed with the
prosecution's contention that any delay would be likely to disperse
the Italian witnesses, many of whom were notoriously unenthusias-

tic over the prospect of testifying against their fellow Italians in Yankee courts. On December 2, 1903, Justice Haselton denied Laird's final motion to delay, and the trial began promptly on Monday, December 14, at 2 PM. Owing to the illness of state's attorney Bailey, the prosecution was led by John H. Senter, who had handled the Garetto case before the grand jury. He was assisted by attorney R. A. Hoar, not without some futile objections on the part of the defense team. Hoar had previously represented Eli Corti's widow and her brother in legal proceedings, but presiding judge Wendell P. Stafford brushed aside Laird's objections and, for good measure, opened the proceedings by appointing John Senter as the new Washington County state's attorney, Frank Bailey having died the weekend before the trial opened. Laird was joined at the defense table by attorneys William A. Lord (the same man who helped defend Mildred Brewster; see chapter 9) and Fred P. Carleton.

The trial's first day saw little drama, consumed as it was in the tedious process of jury selection. There was a poignant moment, however, as Eli Corti's widow, Maria, took her seat in the courtroom. Spotting Alessandro Garetto as she walked past him, she began to cry softly, her body shaking with sobs as her friends tried to quiet her. As with all the trial sessions over the next week, the courtroom was crowded to capacity or beyond, many of the spectators from the Barre Italian community.

John Senter's case for the prosecution was a workmanlike legal presentation, straightforward and untheatrical. His trifold purpose was to prove that Eli Corti had been shot to death, that Alessandro Garetto had shot him, and that he had done so with the conscious intent of killing him. After the jury was completed at 10:35 on Tuesday morning, Senter put Dr. Ligouri on the stand. He was followed by Drs. Chandler, Lindsay, McGuire, and Sweeney. All four physicians, all of whom had treated Eli Corti or participated in his autopsy, testified that Corti had died of an abdominal gunshot wound, the death caused as much by shock as the actual physiological damage. During the cross-examination of Dr. Ligouri, the defense tried to score some points, noting that Corti's autopsy had disclosed evidence of disease in his lungs, left kidney, and brain. But Ligouri held firm to the consensus that Corti's death was caused by a bullet, and the prosecution moved on to establishing motive.

Over a hundred witnesses eventually testified at the trial. It was hard then for impartial observers to tell which witnesses were probably lying—and it is quite impossible to do so now. Strangers in a strange land, the Italians who testified during that long December week had much to be fearful of in this American court. Most of them didn't understand the language used by the officials, and some of them didn't even trust N. J. Ghilarducci or Silvia Origo, the two interpreters furnished by the court. Indeed, it took three interpreters to get orator G. M. Serrati through his testimony; distrusting the two available, he insisted on bringing along his own. Moreover, there were the continuing political hatreds that had spawned the Labor Hall tragedy in the first place. As in the grand-jury proceedings, most of those who testified were known socialists or anarchists, and the character of their testimony and what they said about the other actors in the riot could be pretty well predicted on the basis of their political identification. A partial exception to this pattern of seeming prevarication, much remarked upon at the time, was the willingness of the anarchists to proclaim their political identity. Anarchism might well be the political love that dare not speak its name in a wider America, but, as the correspondent for the *Barre Daily Times* noted, it was flourishing in the Granite City: "It is a somewhat surprising fact," he wrote, "that all anarchists thus far examined have not attempted to dodge the question as to whether or not they belong to that clan. In fact, some have answered, 'yes' with what might be called a proud ring in their voice."

Notwithstanding the impenetrable fog of bilingual perjury, the prosecution gamely tried to set forth the known facts of the killing and Garetto's probable motive. But although Luigi Cassi swore he had seen Garetto making movements as if about to draw a gun, no one testified that they had seen him shoot Corti. True, the defense virtually conceded that Garetto had fired the fatal bullet, but its lawyers bitterly contended that he had fired the shots in self-defense as he attempted to escape the brutal assailants who threatened his life. And the rival witnesses left the jurors little middle ground to choose: Either they were to believe that an unmolested Garetto had fired at Corti out of premeditated spite, or that the badly beaten, disoriented, and terrified socialist had shot to save his life.

The proven facts of the head injuries Garetto suffered on the night of October 3 probably helped him with his jury. But grocery clerk Fritz Jackson's testimony, given on Tuesday, December 17, did not. It was just forty-five minutes to an hour before the shooting, Jackson testified, that Garetto had purchased the box of .32 caliber bullets found on him at the time of his arrest. True, the box had not been opened, but its presence on his person didn't speak well for Garetto's frame of mind as he sauntered off to a partisan political event. And it was not proven one way or the other as to whether Eli Corti played the unlucky peacemaker or the pummeling thug that tempestuous evening. In any case, at least one of the Corti clan was not a probable pacifist: Joseph Bernasconi testified that after Eli Corti was shot, William Corti accosted him and exclaimed, "If my brother dies, you won't live another hour!"

Oddly enough, the only legal cheap shot at the trial was delivered by the defense, rather than the prosecution. One of the principal witnesses against Garetto was the other man he had fired at, Emilio Vochini. Defense counsel Laird worked hard to undermine Vochini's credibility with the jury, implying but not proving that he had a previous criminal record. The highlight of Laird's scorching but ineffectual cross-examination came when he asked the anarchist, "Do you believe in God?" The question was quickly disallowed by Judge Stafford.

Garetto himself did not testify in his own behalf, and the last of the innumerable and contradictory witnesses appeared on Tuesday, December 22. Then Hoar opened the closing argument for the state, stressing the strongest elements of the prosecution's case: the testimony of the four doctors, the premeditation implied by Garetto's timely cartridge purchase, Cassi's testimony about Garetto's suspicious motions, and the defendant's unwillingness or inability to explain what had happened to the murder weapon. Referring scornfully to Garetto's insistence that he was trying to flee his attackers, Hoar wondered skeptically how he was able to get out his gun and aim it with lethal effect when so briskly occupied.

Laird followed with a good effort for the defense. Noting that the state's own witnesses had attested to Garetto's significant head injuries, Laird cited them as powerful support for Garetto's belief that his life was in mortal danger when he fired his revolver. It was, Laird insisted, a case of pure and simple self-defense—unless you believed the state's risible contentions that Garetto fired "without the slightest provocation, that there was no disturbance in the hall that night previous to the shooting, no fighting, and that all was peaceable."

Lord came next, reiterating the weakness of the state's case for premeditation and imploring the jurors to give Garetto's wife and young daughter a Christmas present they would never forget. Then Senter closed for the state, offering a final, dispassionate summary of the case and reminding the jurors that Alessandro Garetto, not the socialists or anarchists of Barre, was on trial. The prosecutor's only appeal to public feeling about the recent immigrant political disturbances was a pointed exhortation that their verdict of guilty be given "in tones loud enough to be heard in Barre."

Judge Stafford's charge to the jury was only thirty minutes long but much to the point. Stating that the defense conceded the fact of the shooting, he instructed them on the law governing Garetto's justification of self-defense. It all came down, he told the twelve in the jury box, to one question: "If the respondent [defendant], when he fired the fatal shot, was being unlawfully assailed by Eli Corti or by Eli Corti in connection with others, and reasonably thought he was in apprehension of death, or was in danger of great bodily harm, he was innocent."

The Garetto jury retired at 9:30 AM on Wednesday, December 23, and returned at 2:50 that afternoon with a verdict of manslaughter. Garetto took the news in silence, as he did Judge Stafford's sentence of not less than ten and not more than twelve years in Windsor Prison at hard labor. Before passing sentence Stafford commented that the verdict indicated the jury had believed that Garetto "was in a passion and that the killing had lacked malice aforethought," much as his defense counsel had contended. An anonymous juror told a reporter that the jury had had little difficulty in settling on the manslaughter verdict.

Everything considered, the aftermath of the Corti killing was better than could be expected. Perhaps chastened or maybe just exhausted by the events of the riot, killing, and trial, Barre's Italian political factions eschewed further provocations and violence. Alessandro Garetto proved to be a model prisoner, valued by Windsor Prison authorities for his handicraft and mechanical skills and even trusted to work on tasks outside the prison walls. He apparently bore no ill feeling against the authorities, telling prosecutor

Senter that he had been much surprised by the fairness and impartiality of his trial. He greeted Senter civilly when the latter visited Windsor Prison in 1906 and two years later sent him a surprise package containing handmade gifts for his family: a handsome picture frame, a woman's sewing rack, and a decorative bottle filled with colored woods.

Garetto's sterling behavior and the unceasing efforts of his partisans to procure him an early release finally paid off in 1909. By that time the passions aroused by the tensions between the Barre factions had cooled and an increasing number of persons had come to believe that perhaps the anarchists had swarmed upon the Labor Hall that night with some malice aforethought. John H. Senter was one of those who signed the petition for Garetto's early release, and he was joined by former chief of police Brown, several current and past Washington County state's attorneys, and seven members of the Garetto jury (the other five were not solicited). On August 4, 1909, Governor George H. Prouty pardoned Garetto, and he returned to Barre.

Like the political passions that led to Corti's killing, the principal surviving actors in his tragedy faded away forever as the years passed. After his return to Barre, Garetto lived there with his family, first at 108 Railroad Street, then at 408 Main Street. According to the account furnished in Mari Tomasi and Roaldus Richmond's *Men Against Granite* (New England Press, 2004), Garetto and his wife eventually returned to Italy, although he shows up in the Barre city directory as late as 1936 before disappearing. Eli Corti's widow, Maria, and her daughters, Emma and Lillian, also remained in Barre for some years, last appearing in the city directory of 1918. There is a faint oral tradition that the families were eventually reconciled, and, as Hemingway would say, wouldn't it be pretty to think so?

CHAPTER 12

THE THETFORD TERROR

The Life and Crimes of George Abbott / Frank Almy, 1857–1893

So they hanged him by
  the neck,
On the gallows, yes, by heck!
So he rests beneath the sod,
For Almy's gone to meet
  his God.

—Contemporary ballad,
circa 1893, said to be
sung to the tune of
"Ta-ra-ra Boom-de-ay"

W as George Abbott Vermont's greatest desperado? His claims to that dubious title are considerable—but any truly impartial judge would have to allow for the rival pretensions of both Massachusetts and New Hampshire in claiming him as a disreputable native son. True, both his father, Harris Abbott, and his mother, Marcia Wilmot, hailed from North Thetford, Vermont, where they grew up as near neighbors in the town dominated by George's grandfather, Eliphalet Abbott, the proud and prosperous proprietor of Abbott's Mills. But need and ambition initially divided them as they came of age in the early 1850s, Marcia securing employment as a loom girl in the mill town of Manchester, New Hampshire, and Harris finding early success as a small businessman in Salem, Massachusetts. In the mid-1850s they met again in North Thetford, and their renewed acquaintance ripened into love. Married in January 1856, they settled in Salem, where their only child, George H. Abbott, was born on January 1, 1857. Harris Abbott did not have long to celebrate the arrival of his son, however, as Marcia died only three days later from complications of

childbirth and soon joined her ancestors in a North Thetford cemetery. Eight days later, George was adopted by his uncle Israel
Abbott and his wife, Mary, and subsequently reared as their son in
Salem until 1857, when Israel moved his family to the old Abbott
property in North Thetford, a handsome estate on the banks of the
Connecticut River. Harris Abbott eventually remarried in Salem,
but Israel and Mary were the only real parents George ever knew.

How can morally decent parents produce depraved offspring?
It is a question as old as the Book of Genesis, and the biography of
George Abbott offers no easy answer. Tradition has it that George
was an attractive boy, well-dressed in a blue suit with brass buttons,
and of pleasing address, especially to members of the opposite sex.
But his character took an early turn to the bad. Academically well-
grounded by his previous study at the Brown School in Salem,
George soon outpaced his fellow students at the Thetford school,
especially in Latin and higher mathematics. He was also an enthusiastic reader, although, tellingly, as one of his early chroniclers
noted, his literary taste ran to "the dime novel order, and only
served to stimulate his evil inclinations." But not long after
George's matriculation, Thetford school authorities became aware
that someone was stealing small objects of value from schoolmates
and teachers, including pens, pencils, and jackknives. Eventually
caught with his stolen loot, George was sent back to school in
Salem, in hopes that the familiar scenes of his childhood might effect a moral reclamation.

They did not. Upon his return to Thetford, he commenced a
career in more serious thievery, stealing jewelry, farm implements,
and tools from his neighbors in the upper Connecticut River Valley.
Conducting his depredations by night, he carefully stashed his loot,
à la Injun Joe of Mark Twain's *Tom Sawyer*, in a cave overlooking
the river. Perhaps the most memorable theft of his tender years

came in 1871, when he purloined a large stove from the dwelling of railroad section hand Daniel P. Prescott near Fairlee. George subsequently fenced the stolen stove to a party in New Hampshire, but owing in part to his already odious reputation, the theft was eventually traced to him, and he was hauled before a Thetford justice of the peace. But thanks to his family's still considerable influence, the case was settled out of court, and George emerged from the toils of the law unpunished and unrepentant. Indeed, his lack of remorse was indelibly demonstrated soon after. One night, while walking on the Abbott acres in North Thetford, he encountered Prescott, accompanied by his beloved dog. Without a word, George whipped out a revolver and shot the dog dead at Prescott's feet. When Prescott remonstrated, George pointed the gun at him and said, "Stop where you are, or I'll treat you just as I did the dog." Having seen enough of the precociously criminal Abbott to know he wasn't kidding, Prescott not only retreated but failed to even report the unprovoked killing of his dog to the authorities. Perhaps he feared the worst from a violent youth who was already known and severely condemned by righteous Vermont folk as a habitual tobacco user.

Doubtless spurred by his seeming invulnerability to consequences, George Abbott accelerated the pace of his burgeoning criminal career. Sometime in the early 1870s he hooked up with his uncle's hired man, ne'er-do-well Peter Duplissy, the vicious scion of a clan described by one Thetford contemporary as a "mess of egg-sucking, doughnut-robbing, cigaroot-smoking scalawags." Operating together and sometimes in company with lesser but sufficiently thuggish accomplices, Abbott and Duplissy commenced a systematic campaign of burglaries in 1874 that terrorized Connecticut River Valley residents from Barnet, Vermont, in the north to Lyme, New Hampshire, to the south. One autumn night the

Abbott-Duplissy gang broke into the home of the Orford town agent, chloroformed him, and made off with ten gallons of liquor and $113 in cash. That same night they burglarized a nearby jeweler's store and the harness shop of H. H. Conant, where they took possession of two revolvers, one hundred keys, a buggy whip, and $1 in cash. Some days later, they returned to Orford, entered the home of jeweler Samuel H. Hale, and absconded with forty silver watches worth $400, twenty gold bosom pins worth $25, and $200 worth of silver watchcases.

Inevitably, given his reputation, suspicions fastened on George Abbott. These suspicions were much aggravated by George's carelessness, which included such professional boners as leaving behind a chisel bearing his uncle Israel's initials during a second robbery of the home of the Orford town agent. Persistent lawmen finally caught up with George, en route to his relatives in Massachusetts, on a train in West Lebanon in the autumn of 1874. When apprehended he was holding a handbag containing a large number of stolen silver watches, two revolvers, a dirk, a bottle of chloroform, a bottle of strychnine, and a bottle of arsenic. On his person he carried another revolver and dirk.

Quickly tried and sentenced, George started his four-year term at the New Hampshire State Prison at Concord on November 5. Back in Salem, Harris Abbott, devastated by his son's disgrace, committed suicide by hanging himself. Perhaps unwisely, his penultimate act was to bequeath a sum of money, at least $3,000, to his errant son upon his coming of age.

George Abbott's first prison experience seemed to signal a change for the better. Conducting himself well, he earned the trust of his jailers, took an earnest part in prison Sunday school exercises, and was rewarded for his model deportment with a reduction of several months in his sentence. Released in 1878, he visited his

Salem kinfolk, collected his legacy, and immediately squandered it on a steam yacht. Several months later he had nothing to show for his inheritance except a photograph of himself attired in a jaunty yachting outfit. Penniless and with no prospects, he drifted back to his uncle's homestead in North Thetford.

To all who inquired about his future, George professed a fervent intention to reform. Placing the blame for his past misdeeds on bad companions and the vulnerability of his tender years, the poetically inclined ex-con warbled high-flown sentiments to family and friends, including this sample filched from Lord Byron and inscribed in a Salem autograph album:

> Oh, talk not to me of names famous in story,
> The days of our youth are the days of our glory;
> And the myrtle and ivy of sweet two-and twenty
> Are worth all your laurel, though it's never so plenty.

Alas, notwithstanding such lofty thoughts, George Abbott was not one of those fated, as Tennyson so acutely put it, to "rise on the stepping-stones of their dead selves to higher things." After working at his uncle's farm for several months, he disappeared from sight. Not coincidentally, about the same time, residents along the upper Connecticut River began to suffer from the very same sort of nocturnal brigandage that had plagued them before Abbott's incarceration. It soon became clear that the recidivist Abbott had recruited a new gang of thieves and was again prosecuting his nightly misdeeds. By November of 1880 lawmen from Lyme to Woodville were searching hard for Abbott and his lair, most likely a hidden cave in the numerous mountains flanking both sides of the Connecticut River. But where?

Abbott's second career as a master burglar came to an abrupt and violent end by accident, although much abetted by his habitual carelessness. Although authorities were planning a general search of the local hills for George's presumed hideout, it was discovered quite by accident by area resident Mark Ware. A former schoolmate of Abbott's, Ware serendipitously spotted him picking apples on Thetford Mountain on Election Day in November of 1880. Discreetly shadowing the unsuspecting Abbott, Ware eventually stumbled upon his robber's cave, which was filled with hundreds of items of incriminating loot and burglar's tools, including a bull's-eye lantern. The lantern, as Abbott chronicler Stewart H. Holbrook has drolly noted, was surely the decisive clue for Ware, for illustrations of bull's-eye lanterns were a stock feature of dime novels, and such a device, "as even the bucolic young Ware must have known, was never carried by anyone except burglars and detectives."

Ware returned to town with his exciting news, and a well-armed posse, led by Thetford sheriff Solon K. Berry, returned to the area of Abbott's cave the next day. Berry, it should be noted, had more than a strictly professional interest in Abbott's capture: On one of his recent nocturnal forays, Abbott had broken into Berry's home and departed with an expensive rifle and $800 in cash. Surprised by Berry's posse, Abbott tried to run for it, shooting at his pursuers as he scrambled through the woods and brush. But they shot back, eventually bringing him down and inflicting no fewer than twenty reported gunshot wounds, most of them on his back.

Seemingly near death from loss of blood and moaning in pain, Abbott was taken on a stretcher to a private residence in Thetford, where he was guarded by Sheriff Berry. But that very night, while Berry was absent answering a call of nature, Abbott made his escape. Clad only in a nightshirt and a blanket, he ran about a mile and a half through the frozen winter landscape before concealing himself in a railroad culvert near the Connecticut River. Four days later a posse of searchers found him there, half frozen but still cocky and defiant. To Berry he boasted that had he not been so weakened by his wounds, he would have swum the Connecticut River and made good his escape. The chastened Berry lost no time in putting his prisoner in the Chelsea jail to await trial. Abbott left the sheriff with this typically vainglorious sentiment, inscribed in his jail notebook and originally authored by James Graham, better known as Montrose, a heroic Cavalier poet and hero of the English Civil War:

> He either fears his fate too much,
>   Or his deserts are small,
> That puts it not unto the touch
>   To win or lose it all.

Briskly convicted on nine counts of burglary, Abbott was sentenced to fifteen years at Windsor Prison and entered on its register as convict 2527. He was further described in that unsentimental record as five feet, eight inches in height, 150 pounds in weight, with hazel eyes, dark hair, a scar over his right eye, judged temperate in the consumption of alcohol but a regular tobacco user.

Once again, George Abbott proved himself a hard man to circumvent. Again conducting himself as a model inmate, he earned the trust of Warden Edwin W. Oakes and other prison officials. Seemingly resigned to his punishment, he worked his way up the prisoner labor hierarchy to a position in the engine room. He took advantage of his hours there to save and secrete lengths of string, cord, and iron pipe and tube. Working for many months, he gradually wove the string and cord into a strong rope ladder, using the metal pieces as makeshift rungs. Biding his time, he waited for the perfect moment.

It came on the evening of September 30, 1887, seven years into his stretch. Part of his job as engine-room attendant was to press a button every fifteen minutes, which rang a bell in Warden Oakes's office. That evening it rang at 7:00, then again at 7:15. It did not ring at 7:30—for in the interval Abbott had hurried to the top of the towering prison wall, thrown his improvised ladder over, and climbed his way to freedom. He would never be seen in Vermont again.

Abbott's whereabouts during the following three years are a murky subject. To begin with, he was no longer George H. Abbott: Like the Count of Monte Cristo, just the kind of fictional hero Abbott admired, the escaped convict obliterated his past in a new identity, christening himself "Frank C. Almy" and henceforth denying any origin or connection with the state of Vermont. Tradition has it that he drifted south, working as a ranch hand in Texas, an oysterman in Baltimore, and an engineer in Savannah. May of 1889 found him laboring as a riveter in Edgemoor, Delaware, under his new nom de plume and claiming New Hampshire as his birthplace. He was next seen at his aunt's home in Cambridgeport, Massachusetts, and subsequently worked as a farm laborer in Peabody.

Over the next year Frank Almy drifted around the rural areas of the Bay State and New Hampshire in a fairly repetitive pattern. Generally employed as a casual laborer, he was known as a steady worker who spent his leisure time reading, had no social life, and was suspiciously reticent about his past. One of the few recorded personal glimpses of Almy in this period comes from Mrs. Caroline Morse, at whose home he boarded while working as an engineer in a Marblehead, Massachusetts, glue factory. While allowing that he was habitually reticent and fond of reading, she deplored his personal habits, which included the smoking of Blackstone cigars and his "peculiar lowery look while eating" her boardinghouse fare. His reading tastes, perhaps inevitably, ran to the escapist genre, including such titles as H. Rider Haggard's *She* and Dumas's *Three Musketeers*.

In July 1890, almost four years after his escape from prison, Almy's aimless drifting brought him to the Hanover, New Hampshire, farm of Andrew H. Warden. Telling Warden he was from Savannah, Georgia, Almy was hired at the rate of $1.25 a day for a week's trial. He soon proved himself an able worker and eventually signed a contract to work for the prosperous farmer through the following March and moved into a room in Warden's comfortable farmhouse. Inevitably, he was thrown into daily contact with the Warden family, which included Warden's wife Louisa, sons Bert and Johnny, and the five Warden daughters: Alice, Myra, Fanny, Susie, and Christie. Alice and Myra soon left for teaching jobs elsewhere, and Fanny, a feisty fifteen-year-old, quickly developed a seething disdain for the new farmhand. Almy had better luck, however, with the twenty-eight-year-old Christie.

One of the ironies of almost all murder narratives is that the murderer usually gets more attention than the victim. And thus it is, however unjust, that we know far more about killer George Abbott/Frank Almy than the person he murdered, Christie Warden. We know that she was a respectable young woman, that she had graduated from the State Normal School, and that she was considered comely and vivacious, if somewhat on the serious side. Described by a contemporary as a "medium-blonde type," she was also said to possess a "fine, rounded form and discreet manners." Serving as the secretary of the Grafton Star Grange, Christie sometimes delivered educational talks at its meetings and also worked part time as a stenographer-secretary for Professor Charles H. Pettee of the State Agricultural College in Hanover. In the wake of her murder, her friends and family made heroic efforts to minimize her attraction to Frank Almy and denied that she had reciprocated any of the volcanic feelings she so undeniably aroused in him. But there is considerable evidence that Frank and Christie drifted into a sort of courtship during his months in the Warden household. There were cozy sleigh rides together, she mended some of his clothes, they attended Sunday services at the College Congregational Church together, he helped her with the housework (ever an infallible sign of abject male infatuation), and they exchanged Christmas presents. The lofty-minded Christie also tried to elevate Frank's lowbrow literary taste, lugging home Edward Bulwer-Lytton's *The Last Days of Pompeii* for improving sessions of reading aloud to each other.

George Abbott could change his name. But he couldn't change his nature, and he couldn't—or wouldn't—contrive a suitably plausible past to go with the relatively genteel persona he tried to present to Christie Warden. Gradually, as the months went by, she detected disturbing character flaws in her swain. His behavior while playing whist was deplorable, and he particularly angered Christie when he successfully bid, contrary to her expressed wish, for a box lunch she had made for a Grange jollification. More disturbing still was Frank's silence about his past, a subject that loomed larger as the months went by and both Christie and Frank sensed her family's largely unspoken but unmistakably chilly disapproval of their growing attachment. During the early months of 1891 Christie left her parents' farm to take a shorthand course in Manchester. While there, she wrote Frank a letter, expressing her reservations about his character and his ominous silence about his past. It was written in a florid style that might have earned the applause of Bulwer-Lytton himself:

> I don't know as you expect an answer to your letters, and perhaps you do not require one, but to be honest with you and true to myself, I think you should know how I feel toward you. You already know, for I have told you, the sort of man I wish to love. . . . You have set yourself in defiance of God and man. I believe

you have suffered the misery that must follow. You surely would not wish me, whom you love, to share that misery.

Since living with us you have not gained my highest regard or respect, nor that of my relatives and friends. Your conduct at the card table has given me more insight into the dark side of your character, of which you have spoken, than any other one thing. . . . I would never think of marrying a man to re-form him. The reformation must come first. I am free to confess that should a man with a clear record desire my love, he would stand a much better chance than yourself. But there are none I know of.

The closing of her judgmental missive, however, extended a feeble hope that Frank could yet earn the love of his good woman:

Frank, I shall test the strength of your love. Can you open your heart to all good influences, practice a rigid self-control and wait patiently? If it is ever so, I believe you must win in the end, for you have many fine qualities that I admire, and I cannot help liking you, with all your faults. . . . I fear I am not worthy of such a love, but I cannot be satisfied unless the man I love is able to become better—for I am weak—rather than to drag me down.

Whatever forlorn hopes Frank nourished of winning Christie's love ended in March 1891. Apparently alarmed by his daughter's attraction to Frank, an alarm probably aggravated by his wife's disquiet about the farmhand and Fanny Warden's more visceral dislike, Andrew Warden gave notice that Frank's contract would not be renewed when it expired on April 1. When that day came, Frank promptly left the Warden home with all his belongings, seemingly bringing an abrupt close to his affair with Christie. She may have left the door open to further communication by letter, but nothing more. Johnny Warden reported to his father that Almy had wept when he bade farewell to the members of the family.

Was Frank Almy planning to return to claim his sweetheart from the moment he left Hanover? It's difficult to be certain, but it was clear that he remained obsessed with her. Returning to Salem, he reclaimed a suitcase of clothing he had left at a boardinghouse before moving on to Boston, where he worked in a Dorchester woodworking shop. While boarding there at the house of Mrs. Michael Quinn, he showed her a photograph of Christie. Remarking it was the girl he loved, he promised, "If I don't have her, then no other fellow will, either."

Sometime in early June of 1891, Frank finally decided to go back and claim Christie as his own. On June 13 he took the train to White River Junction, and that evening he walked up the railroad tracks to Norwich and then across the bridge to Hanover. Taking the Lyme Road north, he arrived at the Warden farm after midnight. Its outbuildings included a series of three interconnected barns, mostly filled with hay from wall to wall. Using a knife to carve out a space in which to sleep, Frank settled down in his new home, just twenty yards away from the bedroom of his beloved. His only possessions were what he had brought with him, mostly presents for Christie: some handkerchiefs, a box of candy, a copy of Rudyard Kipling's just-published *The Light That Failed*—and two revolvers.

However botched its execution, Frank's plan was quite simple. His belief was that if only he could get Christie alone, he could use all the sweet persuasion at his command to induce her to share his life and abjure the family that had poisoned her mind against him. Perhaps she would even agree to his latest fantasy of going off to Texas to start a new life with her in the West. The trick was to get her alone—and this proved to be an almost insurmountable problem. During his long criminal apprenticeship, Frank Almy had become quite adept at skulking around without being seen, and it served him well in his current surveillance of the Warden household. Disguised by a full beard he had grown for the task, he was not even recognized during his furtive nocturnal trips into Hanover or even on the few brief occasions when his face was spotted peering into the windows of the Warden house. Nor did the Wardens or their neighbors become unduly suspicious when the eggs from their chicken coops, milk from their milk cans, and fruit from their orchard trees began to disappear, filched by Almy on his nightly forays for provisions. But try as he might, Frank could not find an occasion when Christie was alone.

As the days crept by, Almy became increasingly impatient. On several occasions he actually sneaked into the Warden house, even running his hands over the keys of the parlor piano as he recalled the nights he had spent with Christie at the instrument as she sang "Listen to the Mockingbird" and other sentimental ditties of the day. One night he even slipped into her upstairs bedroom, only to find her brother Johnny asleep in her bed, before he fled undetected. Some days later, on July 15, he discovered that she was spending that night in Hanover, at the home of her employer, Professor Pettee. Frank decided to surprise her there, perhaps spurred on by jealous, if unfounded, suspicions of the professor. The initial surprise was equally Frank's, however—for after he climbed a ladder to the second-floor bedroom of the residence on North Park Street and entered through a window, he found himself confronting another Pettee guest in her bed, a Miss Amelia Thompson. Seizing the terrified woman by the throat, Frank threatened to kill her if she told anyone of his visit. Placing a revolver cartridge in her hand, he warned her to think about it whenever she was tempted to talk about his visit. Understandably, if unfortunately for Christie Warden, Miss Thompson kept her promise only too well.

Two days later, Frank's opportunity finally came. From his hiding place in the barn he could peer through a knothole and see and hear everything occurring in the vicinity of the Warden house. Learning that Christie would attend a Grange meeting that night, he later slipped out of the barn and staked out the Grange Hall. His chance seemed to come when he saw a girl dressed as Christie had been earlier. She was walking with a young man, and the enraged Frank accosted them from behind and put his hand on her shoulder, crying, "Here, this is a pretty piece of business!" The girl spun around—only to reveal herself as Miss Lottie Kellogg, a friend of Christie Warden's. Realizing his mistake, the abashed Almy ran away and hid himself.

It was about 9:15 that evening when a party of four women came walking down the Lyme Road toward the Warden farm. They were Louisa, Christie, and Fanny Warden, returning from the Grange meeting and accompanied by their friend Louisa F. Goodell. It was a particular charming area, known to the local residents as the Vale of Tempe—a fanciful classical reference to a spot at the foot of Mount Olympus said to be a favorite resort of Apollo and the nine muses.

It happened so fast it must have seemed like a nightmare to the four women. Suddenly, a strange, bearded man jumped out in the road in front of them and began shouting. Brandishing a Smith & Wesson six-shot .44 caliber revolver, he said to Louisa, "Mrs. Warden, you know me. I'm Frank Almy. I only want to talk to Christie. The rest of you run along. You go on and I won't hurt you. If you interfere with me I will shoot you like dogs." Too terrified to move or speak, the women initially stood silent and unmoving. Turning to Christie, Almy grabbed her by the arm and said, "Christie, I have come a thousand miles to see you."

Frank had hoped to see Christie when Fanny wasn't present, and his desire had been a prudent one. Grabbing Christie's free arm, Fanny tried to pull her away from him, and the reluctant threesome struggled for some moments in the road. Tiring of the pulling match, Frank stuck the muzzle of his revolver against Fanny's head and hissed, "I hate you, Fan. Unless you go, I'll kill you." It is reported, however improbably, that the doughty Fanny riposted in language that would have pleased her sister's favorite authors: "I know it, but whatever you do, Frank, be a gentleman." Struggling in his grip, Christie responded in flowery kind, "Don't hurt Fanny! If you do, we must part forever."

Eventually, Frank's superior strength prevailed. Clasping Christie by the waist, he dragged both girls with him as he struggled toward the gates of a fence at the side of the road. Stumbling along in the dark, Fanny tripped, and her sister slipped from her grasp. Dragging Christie through the fence, Frank pulled her by her skirts toward a clump of willows by a brook where there was a small meadow. Fanny pursued them, hearing the screams of her sister as she vainly tried to escape from her captor. At first Christie cried, "Frank, let me go. This is outrageous." But by the time he got her to the meadow, she was screaming, "Oh, Fanny, come and help me. He is tearing my clothes all off!"

Fanny Warden was a remarkably brave girl. Refusing to abandon her imperiled sister, she doggedly pursued Frank and his captive across the field, eluding the three shots he fired at her in the dark. Finding her efforts futile, she scurried back to the road and told her mother and Miss Goodell to go for help. Running up the hill toward Hanover, Miss Goodell met Emmett Marshall, a local farmer who was also returning from the Grange meeting. Fanny led him to the meadow. They arrived in time to hear two more shots fired, and then saw Almy sprint up an adjoining hill and disappear into the brush.

In the grass under the willow trees it was all over for Christie Warden. It will never be known whether Frank Almy raped her or whether he even tried. Nor is it known whether he even attempted to persuade her to go away with him. Whatever happened between them, it ended when he shot her in the head, killing her instantly. Judging from the powder burns later found on her face, he put the revolver right to her head before firing. His second shot, fired when she was already dead and lying on her back, went through her vagina, effectively destroying any evidence of rape and, at the least, indicating considerable spite on Almy's part.

Marshall soon summoned aid from Hanover, but there was little to be done for the unfortunate Christie but organize her obsequies. Attention therefore immediately shifted to the hunt for her killer. Within hours, hundreds of armed men, including many Dartmouth College professors and students, were searching every possible hiding place within a twenty-mile radius of Hanover. A reward fund, eventually amounting to $5,000, was posted. Wanted posters were quickly prepared and sent out to all New England states, with special attention to sites where Almy might try to escape into Canada. As usual in such manhunts, the most immediate fruit of such efforts was a rash of false sightings. These included an unfortunate drifter arrested in Hartford, Vermont, another "suspicious" man apprehended in Sharon, Vermont, and a third suspect jailed in Montpelier by a jubilant Sheriff E. W. Howe, who expressed smug certainty that he had the right man. Even more illusory Green Mountain glimpses of Almy occurred in West Olcott Falls, Derby Line, Newport, Bellows Falls, Sherbrooke, Corning, and Plainfield. He was also seen in Connecticut, Massachusetts, and New York, not to mention just about every town in New Hampshire. Just two days after the murder, he was also spotted in Montreal, Canada, allegedly booking passage for England. None of the reported sightings proved valid, leaving many thoughtful observers to conclude that Almy had either drowned accidentally while escaping or committed suicide somewhere in the pathless woods of the White Mountains.

He had not. Amazingly, like some human purloined letter, Almy had baffled his legion of pursuers simply by *remaining near the scene of the crime*. Rendered shocked and despondent by his deed, he had immediately sought refuge in his secret hiding place in Andrew Warden's commodious hay barn. There, peering through his convenient knothole, he had a bird's-eye view of the events occurring after Christie's death. These included the manhunt for him and Christie's funeral, which took place on the afternoon of July 20. Sitting quietly during the daylight hours in his hollowed-out cave of hay, Almy would emerge every night after dark to steal eggs, canned goods, and other victuals from the cellars and chicken coops and orchards of Hanover residents, not excepting his host family. Sometimes he even sneaked into Hanover, and he visited Christie's grave several times, placing flowers on it and even planting a small tree nearby in her memory. And thus a month elapsed, the trail of Miss Warden's killer growing ever fainter.

There was still a minority opinion, however, shared by a few lawmen and civilians, that Frank Almy had never left the Hanover area. But no one paid much attention to such voices until Monday, August 17. Late that afternoon, Mrs. Louisa Warden came to the barn in quest of some fugitive chickens. She didn't find them—but while poking around the hay barn for their presumed hiding place she discovered a small opening by the foundation that had been concealed with a piece of board. Inside the hole she discovered an empty jelly jar, empty beer bottles, and perhaps a dozen cans that had once contained fruit, salmon, sardines, peaches, and oysters. After she alerted Grafton County solicitor William H. Mitchell and Lisbon sheriff Silas H. Brigham, further searches were prosecuted the next day. They turned up more empty cans, jars, and a birch limb that had been whittled into the shape of a rather impressive billy club. Andrew Warden even turned up the remnants of Almy's moustache, which he had shaved off and discarded in a paper. The search was on in earnest again.

That Wednesday night, August 19, Professor George H. Whitcher of the State Agricultural College and Deputy Sheriff H. C. Brown staked out the Warden barn. Sure enough, as they watched hidden in an adjacent cornfield, they saw a shadowy figure emerge from the barn about 2 AM. They weren't close enough to tell whether it was Almy, but it had his gait, and the figure crept warily to an apple orchard near them and picked apples off the trees and put them into a bag. Whatever the man's identity, he was clearly barefoot, raggedly clad, and remarkably thin. He then retraced his steps toward the barn, disappearing from sight around its east end.

Brown and Whitcher weren't sure that it was Almy or whether he had even reentered the barn. But they were sufficiently convinced to run to Hanover, where they soon recruited a posse of some forty men. Returning to the Warden barn, the men began searching it methodically with pitchforks. By daylight, the Dartmouth Hall bell and church bells throughout the region were ringing the alarm, summoning area residents to join the force now surrounding the barn.

The denouement of the Almy hunt proved more farce than drama. Although possibly as many as a thousand men—nastily characterized by the *Lebanon Free Press* as the "curious, the do-nothings, and the fault finders"—participated in searching the barn, the hours passed with no trace of the killer. Indeed, some searchers became so impatient with the lack of progress that they suggested the barn be set on fire—the method that had famously brought John Wilkes Booth to bay. But calmer heads prevailed, and so it took until 8 AM before Almy was run to earth. One of the searchers, Charles E. Hewett, was a summer student at the State Agricultural College in Hanover, and he had a gun in his pocket. He and searcher Joe Lovell had been poking at the hay for some time when, without warning, Lovell's shovel hit something unyielding. "I've struck him," announced Lovell. As if to prove his claim, the next sight he saw was Almy rising out of the hay. He was shooting as he came, and one of the bullets hit Lovell's shovel, causing him to flee. But Hewett, who was well acquainted with Almy, stood his ground, crying, according to his own colorful recollection, "Frank Almy! You villain!" Almy shot several times at Hewett and missed, barely creasing Hewett's nose with one bullet. The cooler Hewett did not miss, hitting Almy at least three times: one bullet creasing his skull, one hitting his left thigh, and one smashing the bone below his left knee. But the game Almy kept shooting, and Hewett was eventually driven off. He returned to the excited searchers outside, delivering what chronicler Stewart H. Holbrook has justly described as "one of the finest pieces of understatement on record in the Granite State": "I guess that man Almy's in this barn."

Two hours of burlesque negotiations now ensued, with Almy making repeated vows to surrender if promised he would not be lynched and would get a fair trial. Several times Hanover selectman John L. Bridgman, Grafton County solicitor Mitchell, and John M. Fuller, the superintendent of the Dartmouth College Farm, emerged from such parleys, triumphantly announcing to the angry, armed crowd that Almy would soon surrender. But Almy repeatedly reneged on such pledges, and it was almost 10 AM before his besiegers finally rushed Almy and hustled him into a waiting carriage. There were some cries of "Lynch him!" and "String him up!" before the carriage left, but the crowd was ultimately receptive to Selectman Bridgman's appeal to their better instincts:

Fellow citizens, Almy has been found. Now I call upon you in the name of law and good order to restrain your anger and let the law take its course with this foul murderer. I say this at the request of the county officials, men whom we chose by our votes to act for us. We all have confidence in them. We have as good courts as there are on the face of the earth.

Bridgman had reason to be grateful that matters had turned out so happily: Hundreds of shots had been fired wildly during the long siege by the excited crowd, and he believed it was a miracle no innocent person had been killed or seriously injured in the careless crossfire. He allowed no credit to Almy for that, as the prisoner told him that if he'd had his way he "would have shot every damned man who stuck his head into that barn."

Hanover lacking a secure jail, Almy's captors took him to the Wheelock House Hotel, where his wounds were dressed by Drs. C. P. Frost, W. I. Smith, and P. S. Connor. The news that Almy had been captured soon attracted a hostile mob of well over a thousand, some of whom voiced threats to lynch him. Concerned that they might get out of hand, Sheriff Bridgman eventually acceded to their demands that they be allowed to see the prisoner. And so, one by one, as if in a receiving line, an estimated 1,500 persons filed up the stairs to Almy's hotel room and gawked at the bloody prisoner until he fainted and Bridgman halted the unseemly public spectacle. In an effort to deter further threats against the prisoner, well-armed guards were posted around the hotel, and Bridgman sent telegrams to the surrounding towns, exhorting authorities to discourage anyone from going to Hanover to view the notorious prisoner.

The wheels of justice now moved fast. The following morning New Hampshire attorney general Daniel Barnard and local officials conducted the preliminary hearing in Almy's room. When asked what his plea was, Almy turned to Hanover deputy sheriff J. T.

Foster, with whom he was acquainted, and said, "I don't know what to do." Acting on the advice of Barnard that "not guilty" was always the safest way to go, Almy then pleaded not guilty and waived examination. Later that day, he granted an interview to a reporter, attempting to put the best possible face on his atrocious crime:

> I know I committed a brutal murder, nevertheless I am not a brute, paradoxical though that statement may appear. I don't deserve any pity and I ought to suffer for my crime. Christie said she loved me, that I had many qualities she admired, and she added, "you must test your sincerity for me by living an upright, manly life and perhaps some time in the future your efforts will be rewarded." I am sure that had there been no outside influence we should have got along much better.

When asked why he not left the Warden barn, he said that he had tried to after he became aware that Mrs. Warden had discovered clues to his hiding place on Tuesday, August 18. But he got only as far as White River Junction before he was irresistibly drawn back to the scene of his crime. He insisted that he had not tried to rape Christie and that her death had been an accident.

Almy's captors soon found themselves in a thorny legal difficulty. Although they desperately wished to remove him to a more secure jail outside Grafton County, they were stymied by a New Hampshire law mandating that no unconvicted prisoner could be held in a jail outside the county where his alleged crime had been committed unless his captors secured a countervailing order from at least two justices of the New Hampshire Supreme Court. That order was finally secured by Tuesday, August 25, and Almy was taken by train to Manchester and incarcerated in a proper jail. But the delay in his removal had expedited at least one beneficial result, which was his positive identification as escaped convict George H. Abbott. From the moment of his capture in the barn, Almy had insisted he was Frank Almy from either New Hampshire or Boston, not George Abbott, and he would insist upon that fiction until his death. And a surprising number of people in Hanover initially put credence in his denials, arguing that it strained credulity to believe that the notorious George Abbott would have returned to an area where he was so well known. But while he recuperated from his wounds in his room at the Wheelock House, a steady stream of old acquaintances dropped by to pay a call, most of whom quickly identified him as George Abbott. They included his old school chum Mark Ware, Windsor Prison warden Oakes, Abbott's maternal uncle Ephraim Wilmot, and two old foes from his Vermont era: Daniel Prescott and Thetford sheriff Solon K. Berry. To skeptics who insisted that Almy could not be Abbott, because of the alleged absence of some scars on the prisoner, Berry had nothing but scorn. "It is rank nonsense," he said, "to say that this man is not George Abbott. Why I could pick him out of a million men. It makes no difference whether the examination shows the supposed small scars or not. He is the man beyond doubt."

As it happened, a more thorough medical examination made before Almy left Hanover found the disputed scars, virtually all of them souvenirs from his numerous tangles with the law.

There was never much question that Frank Almy was going to be put to death for the murder of Christie Warden. He took advantage of the confusion over where to keep him by deliberately reinjuring his broken leg during a trip from Woodsville to Manchester. But his trial couldn't be indefinitely delayed, and the intense and lurid newspaper publicity about the circumstances of Christie's killing had inflamed the citizens of Grafton County to an unprecedented degree. Hanover resident Professor William T. Smith doubtless spoke for the wider community when he demanded that

Almy be removed from his town: "We don't want this man here—
this monster in crime, who is a lie to himself and a lie to everybody
else. His very presence pollutes the atmosphere and he should
speedily be put in the place provided for such as he."

Even before Almy went on trial, it was clear that nothing was
too awful to credit when it came to his character. Brattleboro's
Vermont Phoenix reported that Fanny Warden, his most implacable
enemy, stated that he had confessed to her family that he had once
killed a relative by hitting him over the head with a chair. "That he
is guilty of this crime," the *Phoenix* blithely editorialized, "is undoubtedly true."

Realizing he had little chance before a Grafton County jury of
Warden neighbors and sympathizers, Almy decided to risk his life
before a two-judge panel, an option available if he were to plead
guilty. On November 16 he did so, and his formal trial opened in
Plymouth the next day before New Hampshire Supreme Court
chief justice Charles Doe and Justice William Henry Harrison
Allen. As he had pleaded guilty, the only legal question to be decided was whether it was first-degree or second-degree murder. A
verdict of second-degree murder might earn Almy up to thirty
years in prison, but a first-degree murder would automatically send
him to the scaffold. Prosecuted by Grafton County solicitor
William H. Mitchell and New Hampshire attorney general Daniel
Barnard, Almy was defended by attorneys Alvin Burleigh and
Joseph C. Story.

Before a rapt audience that packed every session of the three-
day trial, the chief actors in the Christie Warden tragedy told their
stories to the two justices. Louisa and Fanny Warden chronicled
Almy's sojourn with their family and the terrible events in the Vale
of Tempe. One reporter covering the trial wrote that during Fanny's

hostile testimony, "Almy's cruel eyes glistened like a serpent." But during Mrs. Warden's testimony, Almy dramatically broke down, sobbing like a child and beseeching Mrs. Warden, "Oh, Mrs. Warden, please tell it all." He wept again as the shredded clothing worn by Christie on the fatal night was entered as evidence. Miss Goodell and Emmett Marshall followed on the witness stand, the latter describing the condition of the body when he found it in a pool of blood.

Notwithstanding Fanny Warden's almost palpable hatred for the prisoner, the most damaging testimony against Almy was given by Dr. C. P. Frost, who had conducted the autopsy on Christie Warden's body. Contrary to Almy's pretrial claim that he had shot Christie to death only after she had been gravely wounded by an accidental discharge of his revolver, the physician told the judges that the first shot had been fired into the head at close range, killing Christie instantly. As to the question of attempted rape, Frost could not give an opinion, as Almy's second, gratuitous shot had been fired into her vagina as she was lying dead on the ground. Frost's testimony was corroborated by Dr. Edwin J. Bartlett, who had assisted at the postmortem.

Several members of the Warden family reprised their testimony as unenthusiastic and unhelpful defense witnesses. Then it was Almy's turn, and he made the most of it for several hours on that long Wednesday afternoon. Shaking with emotion and frequently breaking down in tears, he said, "I loved Christie and thought the world of her." He insisted that she had returned his love, and he swore that she had agreed to become his wife, although there was not a shred of evidence to support such an assertion. Desperately groping for an extenuating justification, he blamed Christie's death on her mother, avowing that Christie had aroused uncontrollable passions in him, and "had Mrs. Warden only spoken one pleasant word to me I should not be here today." His version of the murder itself differed little from the accounts of Fanny, Louisa, and Miss Goodell, save his implausible denial that he had meant to shoot Christie:

> When I laid her down, some sort of convulsive movement was made—in some way, I don't know how, the revolver was discharged; I don't know how she was wounded. It flashed through my mind that she was mortally hurt. I raised myself to my feet. What shall I do? I had killer her! Oh, God! O, Christie, forgive me!

Detailing his bizarre odyssey after her killing, Almy opined that his inability to leave the Hanover area was due to his disbelief that his beloved was really dead.

Following Almy's dramatic appearance, several witnesses testified as to Almy's behavior during the interval after he left the Warden farm, focusing on his repeated declarations to others of how he loved Christie and his rather more equivocal hints of starting a new life in Texas. By Thursday, November 19, all the evidence and testimony were finished, and the final arguments began. Interestingly but no doubt properly, Justices Doe and Allen had not permitted attorneys from either side to present any evidence touching on the real identity of Frank Almy. In their closing arguments, Story and Burleigh tried to convince the judges that Almy had not meant to kill Christie and that he had returned merely to claim her as his willing bride and light out for Texas. Their insistence on this improbable explanation only opened the door for Attorney General Barnard's persuasive jeers at the defendant's furtive, dishonest, and unmanly behavior: "What occasion was there for him to come to Hanover on the midnight train, and take up a position in the barn, instead of entering the home of the family? Why did he not write to Christie, as was the understanding at parting? If his purposes were honorable, why should he hide?"

No one was much surprised that Thursday afternoon when Justices Doe and Allen returned after only one hour of deliberation with a verdict of guilty. Given Almy's expressed apathy about the outcome and security concerns about his continuing presence in Plymouth—he had been hanged in effigy within sight of his cell window the night before his trial commenced—the justices made the unusual decision to take him to the State Prison in Concord before the verdict was announced. Almy was not even present to hear himself sentenced to be hanged by the neck until dead on the first Tuesday of December 1892. Nor was he told that he must die until almost a week later.

Owing to legal technicalities, especially judicial qualms about his absence from the courtroom when sentence was pronounced, Almy's execution was delayed. Indeed, these concerns became so great that a second trial, virtually identical to the first, was held in April 1892 and resulted in an identical verdict. Almy's attorneys battled on but met their final defeat on July 28, when the New Hampshire Supreme Court upheld the constitutionality of Almy's death verdict.

George Abbott/Frank Almy was undoubtedly a consummate villain. Still, he comported himself in his final appearance with a dignity much in contrast to most of his previous life. On Tuesday, May 16, a crew hurriedly erected the gallows in the Concord prison yard. After consuming the proverbial hearty breakfast (steamed eggs, rolls, and coffee), he chatted briefly with the prison chaplain and other officials. He was carefully dressed in a black suit and wore a plain gold band, which he claimed had been given to him by Christie as a token of her love. It is reported that he declined to discuss religion with the chaplain but did express considerable doubt about a future life. Cautioned that he would not be allowed to address the invitation-only crowd of 150 persons assembled to see him hang, he declined to make a last statement, and the ghastly procession to the scaffold commenced at 10:13 AM. Climbing the steps of the gallows, he swayed slightly as he gazed in fear at the rope above. Steadying himself, he watched passively as his hands and feet were pinioned, asking Grafton County sheriff C. O. Hurlbert twice in a faint voice whether he could now speak. Hurlbert shook his head and put the rope over Almy's neck and adjusted it carefully. Almy was still pleading to speak when the black hood was pulled over his face and Hurlbert made the final adjustment of the noose. Moments later the trap was sprung and Almy plunged downward.

Like many a hanging, Almy's sendoff was badly bungled. The rope, seven-sixteenths of an inch thick and previously used to hang Portsmouth murderer James Palmer on May 1, 1899, had been carefully tested prior to Almy's hanging and was said to come from the same rope lot used to hang the 1886 Haymarket anarchists. Apparently, however, some of the coils in the knot slipped badly, and when Almy went through the drop his feet hit the floor and his knees bent in view of the horrified crowd. It could clearly be seen that the rope was pulled up over the left ear and the knot was at least a foot above the neck. The deputies in his hanging crew immediately hauled up the rope, and he died, in any case, without any perceptible struggling or suffering. He was pronounced dead after fourteen minutes, and the physicians conducting his autopsy insisted that he had died instantly when his neck snapped between the second and third vertebrae. A defensive Sheriff Hurlbert insisted that the execution had been "perfect." And at least two other eyewitnesses of Almy's death were likewise satisfied: Bert Warden and Charles E. Hewett. When warned that watching the execution of his sister's killer might be a trying ordeal, Bert had replied, "Not so for me. Why, I'd like to be the executioner myself."

Call him what you will, George Abbott/Frank Almy left no legacy, save an unsavory reputation. In accordance with his anguished last request, his body was given a decent burial in the prison potter's field in Blossom Hill Cemetery, and his corpse was spared the potential indignities he feared from curious medical students. A cranky lady in Brockton, Vermont, insisted for some time to credulous reporters that her niece had married Almy during one of his unscheduled prison furloughs, bearing his son before being abandoned by the footloose wanderer. And the $4,000 reward money for his capture was eventually dispersed, after much haggling over its proper recipients. Perhaps ironically, or maybe simply justly, Louisa Warden collected $500 of it—the reward for her discovery of the telltale barn refuse. The remainder was divided equally between the two men who had spotted Almy during his apple-picking foray on the night before his capture, H. C. Brown and Professor George Whitcher. Christie Warden still sleeps in a Dartmouth Cemetery, but the scene of her death has long since become part of a golf course. It's just as well: Several months after the murder occurred, a reporter visited the Vale of Tempe site and noted that every leaf and twig had been stripped by ghoulish souvenir-hunters, some of whom had even stripped the bark off the trees and carved their names.

REFERENCES AND BIBLIOGRAPHY

Vermont historians and antiquarians will doubtless note what is not necessarily obvious to less specialized readers: The stories in this collection are based largely on newspaper accounts, legal documents, judicial accounts, reference books, archival materials, and secondary publications by writers and scholars. For those interested in retracing the trail of my researches I would recommend most especially the Vermont History Center in Barre and the Vermont Department of Libraries in Montpelier. Their matchless resources pertaining to all things Vermont are too copious to enumerate here, but I am particularly indebted to the latter's collection of microfilmed newspapers, including their runs of the *Barre Daily Times, Barre Montpelier Times Argus, Bellows Falls Times, Bennington Banner, Bradford United Opinion, Brattleboro Reformer, Burlington Clipper, Burlington Daily News, Burlington Free Press, Hardwick Gazette, Montpelier Argus & Patriot, Montpelier Evening Argus, Montpelier Vermont Watchman & State Journal, Randolph News & Herald, Rutland Herald, Springfield Reporter,* and *Woodstock Vermont Standard.* I was also fortunate to be able to access ancient issues of the *New York Times,* courtesy of the Cuyahoga County Public Library in Parma, Ohio, whose data banks also furnished crucial entrée to U.S. federal census records. Fellow enthusiasts of Vermont's darker side will doubtless discern the debt this book owes to author Joseph A. Citro's pioneering researches into Vermont weirdness. His books have not only hugely entertained the contemporary audience for Green Mountain dismalia but done much to create it. I have found these titles especially inspiring and useful: *Cursed in New England: Stories of Damned Yankees* (Globe Pequot, 2004); *Green Mountain Ghosts, Ghouls & Unsolved Mysteries* (Houghton Mifflin, 1994); *Green Mountains, Dark Tales* (University

Press of New England, 2001) and *Passing Strange: True Tales of New England Hauntings and Horrors* (Houghton Mifflin, 1997). The following publications were also particularly useful in compiling these individual stories:

CHAPTER 1

Perry, Christina. "Deviant Women: Murder, Justice and Womanhood in Early Vermont History" (thesis, Middlebury College, 1996; copy in Special Collections Department, Bailey/Howe Library, University of Vermont, Burlington).

Sanford, Gregory. "From Ballot Box to Jury Box: Women and the Rights and Obligations of Citizenship" (talk delivered to the Vermont Judicial Historical Society, Addison County Courthouse, Middlebury, June 23, 2000; a copy of Sanford's address may be found on the Internet at: http://vermont-archives.org/talks/jury.html).

CHAPTER 3

Krauss, Clinton. "Blood Calls for Vengeance!: The History of Capital Punishment in Vermont." *Vermont History,* Winter–Spring 1997.

Merulin, Craig, and William F. Rugg. *Capital Punishment in Vermont.* Burlington, VT(?), publisher unknown, 1974.

Smith, Gene. "In Windsor Prison." *American Heritage,* May–June 1996, 100–9.

CHAPTER 5

Dodson, James. "The Haunting Case of Orville Gibson." *Yankee* magazine, December 1987, 74–78, 142–50.

See also articles in *Life* magazine, "A Farm Town's Haunting Sense of Guilt," November 2, 1959, 31–34; "A Second Round in a Village Mystery," June 6, 1960, 64.

For an interesting fictional treatment of the Gibson murder, see Goldberg, Gerald J., *The Lynching of Orin Newfield* (Ballantine